MW00711977

# ACTIVITIES *for*
# SPREADSHEETS

**Minta Berry**

SettingPace
Cincinnati, Ohio

**JOIN US ON THE INTERNET**
WWW: http://www.thomson.com
EMAIL: findit@kiosk.thomson.com     A service of I(T)P®

South-Western Educational Publishing
*an International Thomson Publishing company* I(T)P®

Cincinnati • Albany, NY • Belmont, CA • Bonn • Boston • Detroit • Johannesburg • London • Madrid
Melbourne • Mexico City • New York • Paris • Singapore • Tokyo • Toronto • Washington

PATHWAYS

Managing Editor:  Carol Volz
Project Manager:  Dave Lafferty
Marketing Manager:  John Wills
Design Coordinator:  Mike Broussard
Development & Production Services: SETTINGPACE
Writing:  Scott Ellis and Bret Nealis

ISBN:  0-538-72030-1

2  3  4  5  6  PN  02  01  00  99  98

Printed in the United States of America

ITP ®

International Thomson Publishing

# TABLE OF CONTENTS

# ACTIVITY 1

# Entering Text/Saving/Undo

## OBJECTIVES

**Estimated Time: 15 minutes**

- Enter text into several cells
- Use Undo function
- Save a file

You are a member of a golf tournament and have been asked to provide a list of people who will be playing. It is expected that more people will enter the tournament as the tournament date approaches. You decide to enter the list in a spreadsheet making it easier to enter changes as the roster grows.

## INSTRUCTIONS

1. Create a new spreadsheet.

2. Key the data shown below as displayed. As you complete each entry, experiment with ways to move the cursor (e.g. TAB, arrow keys, and ENTER).

3. Replace *Apple* in cell B3 with **Peach**. Use the Undo feature to change the name back to *Apple*.

4. Save the spreadsheet as ACT001.

5. Close the file.

|    | A | B | C | D |
|----|---|---|---|---|
| 1  | Duffer's Golf Tournament Roster | | | |
| 2  | First Name | Last Name | Street Address | |
| 3  | Jonathan | Apple | 17 N. Cobbler | |
| 4  | Lloyd | Copas | 1648 Glensprings Drive | |
| 5  | Vickie | Ingels | 4890 King Court | |
| 6  | Annette | Janson | 781 White Avenue | |
| 7  | Clancy | Lopez | 6241 Knight Court | |
| 8  | Jack | Nickels | 7777 Washington Blvd. | |
| 9  | Mary Ellen | O'Hearn | 113 Stillwater Path | |
| 10 | Renee | Pomeroy | 6791 Hollister Road | |
| 11 | Chang | Tseng | 1623 Whispering Winds | |
| 12 | Stanford | Underwood | 10 New Bluff Road | |
| 13 | Glen | Voss | 567 Main | |

# ACTIVITY 2

# Entering Text/Saving/Closing

## OBJECTIVES

**Estimated Time: 15 minutes**

- Enter text into several cells
- Save a file
- Close the spreadsheet

Your chemistry class is starting to study the periodic table. You are using the spreadsheet to keep a list of the element names, atomic numbers, and symbols.

## INSTRUCTIONS

1. Create a new spreadsheet.

2. Key the data below as displayed. As you complete each entry, experiment ways to move the cursor (e.g. TAB, arrow keys, and ENTER).

3. Save the spreadsheet as ACT002.

4. Close the file.

|    | A | B | C |
|----|---|---|---|
| 1  | Element | Atomic # | Symbol |
| 2  | Hydrogen | 1 | H |
| 3  | Helium | 2 | He |
| 4  | Lithium | 3 | Li |
| 5  | Beryllium | 4 | Be |
| 6  | Boron | 5 | B |
| 7  | Carbon | 6 | C |
| 8  | Nitrogen | 7 | N |
| 9  | Oxygen | 8 | O |
| 10 | Fluorine | 9 | F |

# ACTIVITY 3 Using GoTo

## OBJECTIVE **Estimated Time:  10 minutes**

• Navigate within the worksheet using GoTo

Your customers are generally located within a three-state region.  To help you remember the various sales tax percentages for each of the three states, you keep a separate section within your worksheet to store the various tax rates.

## INSTRUCTIONS

1. Use the GoTo key to move to cell T100.
2. In cell T100 key Indiana.
3. In cell T101 key Kentucky.
4. In cell T102 key Ohio.
5. In cell U100 key .05.
6. In cell U100 key .06.
7. In cell U100 key .055.
8. Save the spreadsheet as ACT003.
9. Close the spreadsheet.

|     | T        | U     | V |
| --- | -------- | ----- | - |
| 100 | Indiana  | 0.05  |   |
| 101 | Kentucky | 0.06  |   |
| 102 | Ohio     | 0.055 |   |

# ACTIVITY 4

# Selecting Ranges

## OBJECTIVE

**Estimated Time: 10 minutes**

• Select a range of cells

You are keeping track of a little league's statistics. Enter the information shown below. Then, learn to highlight the cells so that you can change the format at a future time.

## INSTRUCTIONS

1. Create a new spreadsheet.
2. Key the data shown below.
3. Highlight the row containing the statistics for Norman Ryan.
4. Highlight cells A2 through C5.
5. Highlight the RBI statistics column.
6. Save the speadsheet as ACT004.
7. Close the file.

|    | A | B | C | D | E |
|----|-----------|------------|---------|------|-----|
| 1  | Last Name | First Name | At Bats | Hits | RBI |
| 2  | Alverez | Marcia | 17 | 6 | 3 |
| 3  | Clark | Susan | 21 | 9 | 7 |
| 4  | Daniels | Frank | 19 | 6 | 2 |
| 5  | Peters | Rose | 21 | 8 | 9 |
| 6  | Reeves | Lance | 12 | 4 | 0 |
| 7  | Ryan | Norman | 18 | 9 | 3 |
| 8  | Stevens | Chris | 16 | 7 | 1 |
| 9  | Topazio | Janet | 16 | 5 | 2 |
| 10 | Tsai | Ming | 20 | 8 | 4 |
| 11 | Vidas | Petros | 22 | 10 | 5 |
| 12 | Webber | James | 17 | 7 | 2 |

# ACTIVITY 5

# Selecting Ranges

## OBJECTIVES

**Estimated Time: 10 minutes**

- Select a row of cells
- Select a column of cells

You are helping the wrestling coach keep track of the wrestlers' weights.

## INSTRUCTIONS

1. Create a new spreadsheet.

2. Key the data shown below as displayed.

3. Highlight the entire row of cells for J. Johnson.

4. Highlight the entire column containing the weights.

5. Save the file as ACT005.

6. Close the file.

|   | A | B |
|---|---|---|
| 1 | B. Torry | 103 |
| 2 | S. Franks | 107 |
| 3 | J. Johnson | 112 |
| 4 | R. Smith | 120 |
| 5 | T. Logan | 135 |
| 6 | B. Holt | 142 |
| 7 | S. Hollis | 157 |
| 8 | D. Rink | 166 |
| 9 | L. Stills | 179 |

# ACTIVITY 6

# Using Range Names

## OBJECTIVES

**Estimated Time: 10 minutes**

- Select a range of cells
- Name a range of cells

You are creating a report that summarizes the commissions of the sales force for your company. Your boss wants to see the summary figures for each quarter.

## INSTRUCTIONS

1. Create a new spreadsheet.
2. Key the data shown below.
3. Select the range B2 through B5 and name the range **Quarter 1**.
4. Select C2 through C5 and name the range **Quarter 2**.
5. Select D2 through D5 and name the range **Quarter 3**.
6. Select E2 through E5 and name the range **Quarter 4**.
7. Save the spreadsheet as ACT006.
8. Close the file.

|   | A | B | C | D | E |
|---|---|---|---|---|---|
| 1 |   | Quarter 1 | Quarter 2 | Quarter 3 | Quarter 4 |
| 2 | T. Salmons | 7563 | 7134 | 7602 | 7511 |
| 3 | E. Stanford | 6398 | 6895 | 6551 | 6478 |
| 4 | C. Freeman | 7195 | 6977 | 7108 | 6983 |
| 5 | J. Archer | 7511 | 7103 | 7555 | 7614 |

# ACTIVITY 7

# Using Save As

## OBJECTIVES

**Estimated Time: 15 minutes**

• Save files
• Save an existing file with a different name

You are required to turn in a monthly expense report to your supervisor. You want to set up a spreadsheet that you can reuse without overwriting data from a previous month. You have decided to create a master worksheet, then save it under a different name at the beginning of each month.

## INSTRUCTIONS

1. Create a new spreadsheet.

2. Key the data shown below as displayed.

3. Save the file as ACT007.

4. Save the file as EXPJAN.

5. Save the file as EXPFEB.

6. Save the file as EXPMAR.

|   | A | B | C | D | E |
|---|---|---|---|---|---|
| 1 |   | Week 1 | Week 2 | Week 3 | Week 4 |
| 2 | Travel |  |  |  |  |
| 3 | Lodging |  |  |  |  |
| 4 | Meals |  |  |  |  |
| 5 | Misc. |  |  |  |  |
| 6 |   |  |  |  |  |
| 7 | Totals |  |  |  |  |

# ACTIVITY 8

# Naming and Saving Documents

## OBJECTIVE

**Estimated Time: 10 minutes**

• Save data files

Saving a worksheet at regular intervals is very important. You should develop the good habit of saving your worksheet every few minutes. Your computer's operating system will allow you to use up to eight alphanumeric characters **plus** the following characters: & ( ) $ ~ _ ^ ! # % - { } @ ` '

You are not allowed to use spaces anywhere within your filename.

## INSTRUCTIONS

1. In cell B2 of a new worksheet key your last name.

2. Save the file as ACT008.

3. Save the file with a name you select. Use at least one of the special characters listed above.

4. Close the file.

# ACTIVITY 9　　　　　　　　　　　　　　　　Editing Cells

## OBJECTIVES　　　　　　　　　　　Estimated Time:  20 minutes

* Use backspace key
* Edit cell entries

　　You are researching the development of the car before the year 1900. As you research, you want to be able to add information to your findings.

## INSTRUCTIONS

1. Create a new spreadsheet.

2. Key the text shown below as displayed. As you enter the text, use the backspace key to correct errors.

3. From your research, you find that the Ford's top speed was 21 miles per hour. Go to cell D5 and add the text **top speed, 21 m.p.h.** after the words "2 cylinder."

4. You also found that the Benz had a horsepower of 1.5. Key **1.5 h.p.** in cell D4 after the words "1 cylinder."

5. Save the file as ACT009.

6. Close the file.

|   | A | B | C | D |
|---|---|---|---|---|
| 1 | Model | Year | Country | Description |
| 2 | Daimler | 1886 | Germany | 1 cylinder |
| 3 | Daimler | 1896 | Germany | 2 cylinder |
| 4 | Benz | 1888 | Germany | 1 cylinder |
| 5 | Ford | 1896 | USA | 2 cylinder |
| 6 | Renault | 1898 | France | 2.25 h.p. |

# ACTIVITY 10 — Editing Cells/Inserting Rows

**OBJECTIVES**

**Estimated Time: 20 minutes**

- Edit cell entries
- Insert a row
- Save an edited entry

Your store is doing a demographic study of the community. You are responsible for recording the findings in a spreadsheet.

## INSTRUCTIONS

1. Create a new spreadsheet.

2. Key the data shown below as displayed.

3. Save the spreadsheet as ACT010.

4. Edit the cell with the year 2000 to read **2000 (Projected)**.

5. You decide to add the following two lines before the Population Income section:

   **Population Average Age**
      33.5    33.0    33.4

6. Save the file.

7. Close the file.

|    | A | B | C | D |
|----|---|---|---|---|
| 1  |                      | 1980   | 1990   | 2000   |
| 2  | Population By Race   |        |        |        |
| 3  | White                | 9,482  | 9,377  | 9,358  |
| 4  | Black                | 8,259  | 9,386  | 10,015 |
| 5  | Hispanic             | 3,566  | 5,612  | 6,836  |
| 6  | Asian                | 1,997  | 3,743  | 4,474  |
| 7  | Population By Gender  |        |        |        |
| 8  | Female               | 12,263 | 14,557 | 15,796 |
| 9  | Male                 | 11,041 | 13,561 | 14,887 |
| 10 | Population Income    |        |        |        |
| 11 | Average              | 15,497 | 24,205 | 28,912 |
| 12 | Per Capita           | 5,958  | 9,284  | 10,974 |

# ACTIVITY 11

# Inserting Rows

## OBJECTIVES

**Estimated Time: 15 minutes**

- Insert blank rows
- Add additional data

You own The Suntan Hut and have recently added a new sunscreen product to your price list. You prefer to insert this new product in the list in such a way as to maintain a logical order. To add the product, you need to insert a blank row.

## INSTRUCTIONS

1. Create a new spreadsheet.

2. Key the data shown below as displayed.

3. Move to cell A4.

4. Insert a new row at row four.

5. In cell A4 key Bronzer SPF 5.

6. In cell B4 key 9.00.

7. In cell C4 key 8.50.

8. In cell D4 key 7.50.

9. Save the file as ACT011.

10. Close the file.

|   | A | B | C | D | E |
|---|---|---|---|---|---|
| 1 |   |   |   |   |   |
| 2 | Product | Qty 1 Price | Qty 10 Price | Qty 25 Price |   |
| 3 | Bronzer SPF 3 | 8.95 | 7.95 | 6.95 |   |
| 4 | Bronzer SPF 8 | 9.95 | 8.95 | 7.95 |   |
| 5 | Bronzer SPF 15 | 10.45 | 9.79 | 8.50 |   |
| 6 | Bronzer SPF 18 | 11.00 | 9.50 | 7.00 |   |

# ACTIVITY 12

# Inserting Columns

## OBJECTIVES

**Estimated Time: 15 minutes**

- Insert blank columns
- Add additional data

You use a worksheet to list your personal expenses for each month.  After you key the column headings for the twelve months, you realize that it would be helpful to total expenses by quarter.

## INSTRUCTIONS

1.  Create a new spreadsheet.

2.  Key the data shown below as displayed.  Continue listing the months through December in row 2.

3   Insert a new column between the existing columns D and E.

4.  In cell E2 key Q1.

5.  Save the file as ACT012.

6.  Close the file.

|   | A | B | C | D | E |
|---|---|---|---|---|---|
| 1 |  |  |  |  |  |
| 2 | Expense | Jan | Feb | Mar | Apr |
| 3 | Rent |  |  |  |  |
| 4 | Equipment |  |  |  |  |
| 5 | Utilities |  |  |  |  |
| 6 | Payroll |  |  |  |  |
| 7 |  |  |  |  |  |

# ACTIVITY 13        Changing Edit Options (Excel Only)

## OBJECTIVES

**Estimated Time: 10 minutes**

- Change view options
- Change the edit options

    You decide to customize Excel to see if you like other options. You want to see what entering data would be like without the gridlines and status bar. You also prefer to use your arrow keys to move from cell to cell when you enter data. Therefore, you want the cell in which you enter data to remain active when you press Enter. Follow the instructions below to see if you like the new options.

## INSTRUCTIONS

1.  Create a new spreadsheet.

2.  In cell A1 key your first name and press Enter. Notice how the active cell is now A2.

3.  Under the Options command, hide the Status Bar and Gridlines and click OK. Notice what has happened to the screen.

4.  Under the Options command, turn off the "Move Selection after Enter." Click OK.

5.  Key your last name and press Enter. Notice that cell A2 remains the active cell.

6.  Press the down arrow to A3 and key your street address. Press Enter.

7.  Press the down arrow to A4 and key your city. Press Enter.

8.  Press the right arrow three times and key your state's abbreviation.

9.  Change the options back to the way they were.

10. Close the file.

# ACTIVITY 14

# Review

## OBJECTIVE

Estimated Time:  30 minutes

♦ Review skills introduced in Activities 1-13

   You need to make comparisons between three cars that are for sale in order to evaluate the one that is the best value for you.  Create a spreadsheet that will be able to be used to input the variables for comparison.

## INSTRUCTIONS

1.  Create a new worksheet.

2.  In cell A1 key **Automobile Comparisons**.

3.  In cell A3 key **Monthly Expense**.

4.  In cell A4 key **Gas**.

5.  In cell A5 key **Insurance**.

6.  In cell A6 key **Payment**.

7.  In cell A8 key **Totals**.

8.  In cell C3 key **Car 1**.

9.  In cell D3 key **Car 2**.

10. In cell E3 key **Car 3**.

11. Use the GoTo key to move to cell A6.

12. Insert a new row at row 6.

13. In cell A6 key **Maintenance**.

14. Key the following values for each car:

| | Car 1 | Car 2 | Car 3 |
|---|---|---|---|
| Gas | 55 | 65 | 40 |
| Insurance | 75 | 68 | 49 |
| Maintenance | 40 | 70 | 55 |
| Payment | 175 | 200 | 185 |
| Totals | 345 | 403 | 329 |

15. Change cell A6 to read **Service**.

16. Change cell A4 to read **Gasoline**.

17. Save the document as ACT014.

18. Close the document.

# ACTIVITY 15 Create Your Own

## OBJECTIVES

+ Enter data
+ Edit cells
+ Save a file
+ Insert a column

In a spreadsheet, you want to keep a directory listing of your friends. Use the skills you have learned to create a list of names and addresses that include columns for last name, first name, street address, city, state, and zip code. After entering several names, you decide that you also want to list phone numbers. These numbers should be next to the first name column so that you can easily look up the number. Insert a column after the first name column and name it *Phone*. Enter the phone numbers in the column.

## INSTRUCTIONS

1. Create a new spreadsheet.

2. Enter your directory listings by inserting at least two names and addresses. Insert the column for phone numbers. Add the phone numbers of the friends whose names and addresses you have already entered. Continue building the directory.

3. Save the file as ACT015.

4. Close the file.

# ACTIVITY 16           Printing a Spreadsheet

## OBJECTIVES

**Estimated Time: 15 minutes**

• Use Page Setup
• Print a spreadsheet

The little league coach would like you to bring the statistics you have been keeping to the game. You need to print the spreadsheet.

## INSTRUCTIONS

1. Open ACT004 that you created in Activity 4. If you did not complete that activity, key the data shown below.

2. Adjust the left margin to 2.5 inches so that the printout will be closer to the center of the page.

3. Print the file.

4. Save the file as ACT016.

5. Close the file.

|    | A | B | C | D | E |
|----|-----------|------------|---------|------|-----|
| 1  | Last Name | First Name | At Bats | Hits | RBI |
| 2  | Alverez   | Marcia     | 17      | 6    | 3   |
| 3  | Clark     | Susan      | 21      | 9    | 7   |
| 4  | Daniels   | Frank      | 19      | 6    | 2   |
| 5  | Peters    | Rose       | 21      | 8    | 9   |
| 6  | Reeves    | Lance      | 12      | 4    | 0   |
| 7  | Ryan      | Norman     | 18      | 9    | 3   |
| 8  | Stevens   | Chris      | 16      | 7    | 1   |
| 9  | Topazio   | Janet      | 16      | 5    | 2   |
| 10 | Tsai      | Ming       | 20      | 8    | 4   |
| 11 | Vidas     | Petros     | 22      | 10   | 5   |
| 12 | Webber    | James      | 17      | 7    | 2   |

# ACTIVITY 17 Printing a Spreadsheet

## OBJECTIVES Estimated Time: 30 minutes

- Specify print ranges
- Print a worksheet

You have been asked to print a list of the ten movies which have earned the most revenues at the box office.

## INSTRUCTIONS

1. Create a new spreadsheet.

2. Key the data shown below as displayed.

3. Specify range A1 to D15 as the print range.

4. Print the worksheet.

5. Save the worksheet as ACT017.

6. Close the worksheet.

|    | A | B | C | D |
|----|---|---|---|---|
| 1  | Top Ten Movies | | | |
| 2  | Total Revenues | | | |
| 3  | | | | Revenue |
| 4  | Movie Title | | Year | in Millions |
| 5  | | | | |
| 6  | E.T. | | 1982 | 228 |
| 7  | Star Wars | | 1977 | 194 |
| 8  | Return of the Jedi | | 1983 | 168 |
| 9  | Batman | | 1989 | 151 |
| 10 | Empire Strikes Back | | 1980 | 142 |
| 11 | Home Alone | | 1990 | 140 |
| 12 | Ghostbusters | | 1984 | 138 |
| 13 | Jaws | | 1975 | 130 |
| 14 | Raiders of the Lost Ark | | 1981 | 116 |
| 15 | Indiana Jones | | 1984 | 109 |

# ACTIVITY 18    Using Print Preview/Changing Page Orientation

## OBJECTIVE

**Estimated Time: 20 minutes**

• Preview a spreadsheet before printing

The chamber of commerce wants more people to take vacations in your city. You are on a committee to monitor attraction attendance figures. These figures will be used to help decide a course of action for future promotions.

## INSTRUCTIONS

1.  Create a new spreadsheet.

2.  Key the data shown below.

3.  Use print preview.

4.  Change the page orientation from portrait to landscape. Select print preview again, if necessary, to view the changed orientation.

5.  Save the file as ACT018.

6.  Close the file.

|   | A | B | C | D | E | F | G | H | I | J | K | L | M |
|---|---|---|---|---|---|---|---|---|---|---|---|---|---|
| 1 | Attraction Attendance Figures | | | | | | | | | | | | |
| 2 | | Jan | Feb | Mar | Apr | May | Jun | Jul | Aug | Sep | Oct | Nov | Dec |
| 3 | Zoo | 64014 | 57784 | 63784 | 78195 | 81322 | 172150 | 272781 | 251211 | 146786 | 135005 | 96899 | 133914 |
| 4 | Museum | 34420 | 31711 | 32378 | 33949 | 33171 | 31221 | 30788 | 29925 | 27755 | 26967 | 26115 | 30156 |
| 5 | Park | 0 | 0 | 0 | 0 | 501489 | 814997 | 1225921 | 1172396 | 869071 | 408934 | 0 | 0 |

# ACTIVITY 19 Printing a Range

## OBJECTIVES **Estimated Time: 30 minutes**

♦ Print a range of data

As a teacher's assistant, you are keeping the grades of the biology class. By keeping the information in a spreadsheet, you can print out only the data the teacher requests.

## INSTRUCTIONS

1. Create a new spreadsheet.

2. Key the information shown below.

3. The teacher requests the grades for Hatcher. Print the range of grades for Hatcher; include Hatcher's full name.

4. The teacher also wants a list of the names of students in the class. Print the range of both last names and first names.

5. Save the file as ACT019.

6. Close the file.

|  | A | B | C | D | E | F | G | H |
|---|---|---|---|---|---|---|---|---|
| 1 | Biology Grades | | | | | | | |
| 2 | Last | First | Quiz 1 | Quiz 2 | Mid-term | Quiz 3 | Project | Final |
| 3 | Abanto | Juanita | 95 | 90 | 97 | 95 | 87 | 93 |
| 4 | Abrams | Laetitia | 90 | 95 | 93 | 90 | 86 | 87 |
| 5 | Baldrick | Glen | 85 | 80 | 89 | 80 | 92 | 84 |
| 6 | Christie | James | 85 | 85 | 88 | 100 | 82 | 90 |
| 7 | Cook | Rodger | 90 | 90 | 94 | 95 | 86 | 97 |
| 8 | D'Adam | Crystal | 75 | 85 | 92 | 90 | 80 | 87 |
| 9 | Fields | Tamera | 95 | 100 | 97 | 100 | 97 | 95 |
| 10 | Harris | Robert | 95 | 95 | 93 | 90 | 91 | 91 |
| 11 | Hatcher | Jeanette | 90 | 95 | 96 | 95 | 88 | 100 |
| 12 | Horwitz | Aaron | 100 | 95 | 97 | 95 | 95 | 95 |
| 13 | Kinney | Sheila | 85 | 95 | 94 | 80 | 86 | 91 |
| 14 | McCaw | Chris | 70 | 75 | 81 | 80 | 81 | 85 |
| 15 | Meece | Henry | 90 | 90 | 97 | 95 | 89 | 92 |
| 16 | Reed | Paul | 80 | 85 | 91 | 95 | 79 | 89 |
| 17 | Schwartz | Janet | 85 | 85 | 93 | 95 | 80 | 84 |
| 18 | Stockton | Mark | 90 | 95 | 88 | 95 | 87 | 88 |
| 19 | Strauss | Lisa | 80 | 85 | 90 | 90 | 91 | 86 |

# ACTIVITY 20

# Creating Headers and Footers

## OBJECTIVES

**Estimated Time: 20 minutes**

* Create a header
* Create a footer

At the conclusion of each day, you need to print a report that shows the number of customer service calls you have handled over the telephone each hour. The report must show your name at the top center, the current date at the bottom left, and the current time at the bottom right of each page.

## INSTRUCTIONS

1. Create a new spreadsheet.

2. Key the data shown below.

3. Create a header that includes your first and last name in the top center of the page.

4. Create a footer that prints the current date flush left and the current time flush right.

5. Save the worksheet as ACT020.

6. Close the file.

|    | A | B | C |
|----|---|---|---|
| 1  | Customer Service Call Log | | |
| 2  | | | |
| 3  | Hour | # of Calls | |
| 4  | 9:00am | 22 | |
| 5  | 10:00am | 18 | |
| 6  | 11:00am | 14 | |
| 7  | 12:00m | 24 | |
| 8  | 1:00pm | 31 | |
| 9  | 2:00pm | 17 | |
| 10 | 3:00pm | 15 | |
| 11 | 4:00pm | 12 | |
| 12 | 5:00pm | 16 | |

# ACTIVITY 21

# Inserting Page Breaks

## OBJECTIVE

**Estimated Time: 30 minutes**

- Insert page breaks into a worksheet

Your company has three stores in the metropolitan area — north, south, and midtown. You wish to print a separate report for each store without specifying three separate print ranges and issuing the print command three times.

## INSTRUCTIONS

1. Create a new spreadsheet.
2. Key the data shown below.
3. Insert a page break in cell A5.
4. Insert a page break in cell A9.
5. Print the range A1 to F12.
6. Save the worksheet as ACT021.
7. Close the file.

|    | A       | B   | C   | D   | E   | F   |
|----|---------|-----|-----|-----|-----|-----|
| 1  |         | Mon | Tue | Wed | Thu | Fri |
| 2  | North   |     |     |     |     |     |
| 3  | Sales   | 100 | 94  | 114 | 120 | 88  |
| 4  | Rentals | 45  | 65  | 71  | 23  | 44  |
| 5  |         |     |     |     |     |     |
| 6  | Midtown |     |     |     |     |     |
| 7  | Sales   | 98  | 77  | 62  | 45  | 59  |
| 8  | Rentals | 44  | 39  | 38  | 49  | 55  |
| 9  |         |     |     |     |     |     |
| 10 | South   |     |     |     |     |     |
| 11 | Sales   | 122 | 133 | 146 | 99  | 152 |
| 12 | Rentals | 87  | 78  | 56  | 62  | 99  |

# ACTIVITY 22            Using Context-Sensitive Help

## OBJECTIVE

**Estimated Time: 10 minutes**

+ Locate help in context

When creating range names, you need help remembering the guidelines and rules. Use the Help system to locate help in context.

## INSTRUCTIONS

1.  Create a new spreadsheet.

2.  Pull down each menu until you find the option for naming ranges. Highlight the option on the menu.

3.  Rather than naming a range at this point, press the Help key to locate help in naming ranges.

4.  Review the help screens to learn the rules for naming ranges.

5.  Close the worksheet without saving it.

# ACTIVITY 23      Using Help to Display Definitions

## OBJECTIVE

**Estimated Time: 30 minutes**

• Display Help Topic definitions

You need some assistance with the various codes that can be used in Headers and Footers to generate the current date, current time, page number, and other features.

## INSTRUCTIONS

1. Create a new spreadsheet.
2. Press the Help key.
3. From the table of contents locate the option that takes you to topics on headers and footers.
4. If possible, print the Help screens on headers and footers to use as a reference.
5. If necessary, navigate further through the system to find specific help on the various codes that can be inserted into headers and footers.
6. Close the worksheet without saving.

# ACTIVITY 24

# Using Help Contents

## OBJECTIVE

* Access Help Contents

You are a computer operator at a small company. There are times during the day that you have to wait for work. You decide to expand your knowledge about spreadsheets during these "down times" by exploring the Help Contents.

## INSTRUCTIONS

1. Create a new spreadsheet.

2. Access the Help Contents menu.

3. Look for help about creating macros.

4. Now look for help about formulas.

5. Explore any other function you find interesting.

6. Close the worksheet without saving it.

# ACTIVITY 25      Creating and Using Horizontal Titles

**OBJECTIVE**                              **Estimated Time: 15 minutes**

♦ Use horizontal titles

You are a sales representative based in Chicago. You are compiling a list of the cities that you travel to throughout the year. You want the distance figures in both miles and kilometers.

## INSTRUCTIONS

1. Create a new spreadsheet.

2. Key the information shown in row 1 on the next page.

3. Set the horizontal titles so that row 1 will always display.

4. Key the remaining information. Notice that as you key the information, the column titles remain on the screen.

5. Save the file as ACT025.

6. Close the file.

|   | A | B | C |
|---|---|---|---|
| 1 | City | Miles | Kilometers |
| 2 | Albany | 836 | 1345 |
| 3 | Albuquerque | 1335 | 2148 |
| 4 | Atlanta | 716 | 1152 |
| 5 | Baltimore | 715 | 1150 |
| 6 | Birmingham | 663 | 1067 |
| 7 | Boise | 1705 | 2743 |
| 8 | Boston | 1015 | 1633 |
| 9 | Buffalo | 546 | 879 |
| 10 | Charlotte | 785 | 1263 |
| 11 | Cleveland | 355 | 571 |
| 12 | Columbus | 361 | 581 |
| 13 | Dallas | 928 | 1493 |
| 14 | Denver | 1011 | 1627 |
| 15 | Detroit | 286 | 460 |
| 16 | Houston | 1085 | 1746 |
| 17 | Indianapolis | 185 | 298 |
| 18 | L.A. | 2034 | 3273 |
| 19 | Louisville | 299 | 481 |
| 20 | Memphis | 536 | 862 |
| 21 | Miami | 1377 | 2216 |
| 22 | Nashville | 474 | 763 |
| 23 | New Orleans | 929 | 1495 |
| 24 | New York | 821 | 1321 |
| 25 | Philadelphia | 772 | 1242 |
| 26 | Phoenix | 1800 | 2896 |
| 27 | Pittsburgh | 472 | 759 |
| 28 | St. Louis | 297 | 478 |
| 29 | San Fran. | 2148 | 3456 |
| 30 | Washington | 715 | 1150 |

# ACTIVITY 26　　　　Creating and Using Vertical Titles

## OBJECTIVE

**Estimated Time: 30 minutes**

◆ Use vertical titles

You are studying the desirability of living conditions in several U. S. cities. One of the factors is climate. You will use a spreadsheet to keep track of your findings. As you move to different columns, the cities' names will scroll off the screen. By creating vertical titles, you will be able to keep the names on the screen.

## INSTRUCTIONS

1. Create a new spreadsheet.

2. Enter the names of the cities in column A shown below.

3. Set the vertical titles so that column A will remain on the screen.

4. Finish keying the data shown below. Notice that the city names do not scroll off the screen as you key data.

5. Save the file as ACT026.

6. Close the file.

|   | A | B | C | D | E | F | G | H | I | J | K | L | M |
|---|---|---|---|---|---|---|---|---|---|---|---|---|---|
| 1 | Average Monthly High Temperatures | | | | | | | | | | | | |
| 2 | | Jan | Feb | Mar | Apr | May | Jun | Jul | Aug | Sep | Oct | Nov | Dec |
| 3 | Chicago | 29 | 34 | 44 | 59 | 70 | 79 | 83 | 82 | 76 | 64 | 48 | 35 |
| 4 | Denver | 43 | 47 | 51 | 61 | 71 | 82 | 88 | 86 | 78 | 67 | 52 | 46 |
| 5 | Honolulu | 80 | 80 | 81 | 83 | 85 | 86 | 87 | 88 | 88 | 87 | 84 | 81 |
| 6 | L. A. | 65 | 66 | 65 | 67 | 69 | 72 | 75 | 77 | 76 | 74 | 70 | 66 |
| 7 | Miami | 75 | 76 | 79 | 82 | 85 | 87 | 89 | 89 | 88 | 84 | 80 | 76 |
| 8 | New York | 38 | 40 | 49 | 61 | 72 | 80 | 85 | 84 | 76 | 66 | 54 | 42 |
| 9 | Seattle | 44 | 49 | 51 | 59 | 64 | 69 | 75 | 74 | 69 | 60 | 50 | 46 |

# ACTIVITY 27

# Creating and Using Titles

## OBJECTIVE

• Use horizontal and vertical titles

You are in charge of stocking hardware items in a chain of stores. You will use a spreadsheet to keep a list of item numbers and how many of each item is sold in each store. Since there are more rows and columns than can be displayed on the screen at one time, you will want to use both horizontal and vertical titles.

## INSTRUCTIONS

1. Create a new spreadsheet.

2. Enter the text in rows 1 and 2 as shown on the next page.

3. Create titles so that both the Item numbers and store numbers will always display.

4. Key the remaining data on the next page.

5. Save the file as ACT027.

6. Close the file.

|   | A | B | C | D | E | F | G | H | I | J |
|---|---|---|---|---|---|---|---|---|---|---|
| 1 | Number of Items Sold Per Store | | | | | | | | | |
| 2 | Item # | Store 1 | Store 2 | Store 3 | Store 4 | Store 5 | Store 6 | Store 7 | Store 8 | Store 9 |
| 3 | NL1002 | 9 | 7 | 2 | 3 | 4 | 7 | 5 | 6 | 7 |
| 4 | NL1003 | 1 | 0 | 2 | 1 | 1 | 0 | 3 | 1 | 0 |
| 5 | NL1004 | 4 | 4 | 3 | 5 | 2 | 5 | 3 | 3 | 2 |
| 6 | NL1005 | 9 | 14 | 12 | 10 | 9 | 12 | 11 | 10 | 12 |
| 7 | SW1001 | 3 | 2 | 2 | 4 | 1 | 3 | 2 | 1 | 1 |
| 8 | SW1002 | 1 | 4 | 2 | 3 | 1 | 3 | 1 | 2 | 2 |
| 9 | SW1003 | 7 | 5 | 7 | 9 | 8 | 9 | 6 | 7 | 9 |
| 10 | SW1004 | 2 | 1 | 2 | 3 | 3 | 1 | 2 | 2 | 1 |
| 11 | SW1005 | 4 | 2 | 5 | 3 | 4 | 1 | 4 | 3 | 2 |
| 12 | SW1006 | 2 | 3 | 3 | 3 | 1 | 2 | 2 | 1 | 1 |
| 13 | SW1007 | 7 | 5 | 4 | 6 | 7 | 7 | 5 | 4 | 6 |
| 14 | SW1008 | 3 | 1 | 2 | 1 | 2 | 1 | 2 | 3 | 1 |
| 15 | SW1009 | 1 | 3 | 2 | 3 | 1 | 2 | 4 | 3 | 1 |
| 16 | SW1010 | 3 | 2 | 1 | 1 | 3 | 0 | 3 | 4 | 6 |
| 17 | SW1011 | 4 | 3 | 4 | 1 | 6 | 2 | 4 | 6 | 2 |
| 18 | HG1001 | 5 | 6 | 1 | 6 | 3 | 6 | 5 | 7 | 4 |
| 19 | HG1003 | 4 | 6 | 4 | 4 | 3 | 5 | 5 | 4 | 3 |
| 20 | HG1004 | 3 | 4 | 3 | 3 | 4 | 3 | 3 | 3 | 3 |
| 21 | HG1005 | 1 | 2 | 2 | 2 | 1 | 2 | 0 | 1 | 0 |
| 22 | HG1006 | 3 | 4 | 3 | 4 | 4 | 3 | 2 | 5 | 4 |
| 23 | HG1007 | 3 | 6 | 4 | 5 | 4 | 5 | 5 | 6 | 2 |
| 24 | HG1008 | 4 | 6 | 5 | 1 | 6 | 4 | 2 | 3 | 4 |
| 25 | HG1012 | 2 | 3 | 1 | 4 | 2 | 3 | 1 | 5 | 3 |

# ACTIVITY 28                    Using Shortcut Menus

## OBJECTIVE                                    **Estimated Time: 30 minutes**

- Use the shortcut menu to insert rows

You have added two new sales representatives to your sales staff and need to include their names alphabetically in your sales tracking worksheet.

## INSTRUCTIONS

1. Create a new spreadsheet.
2. Key the data shown below as displayed.
3. Move to row 6 and use the shortcut menu to insert a new row.
4. In cell A6 key **Gwyn**.
5. Now, move to row 8 and use the shortcut menu to insert a new row.
6. In cell A8 key **Marie**.
7. Save the worksheet as ACT028.
8. Print the spreadsheet.
9. Close the file.

|   | A | B | C | D | E |
|---|---|---|---|---|---|
| 1 | Sales Record | | | | |
| 2 | | | | | |
| 3 | Rep | Jan | Feb | Mar | |
| 4 | Bryan | | | | |
| 5 | Bridget | | | | |
| 6 | Malorie | | | | |
| 7 | Robert | | | | |

# ACTIVITY 29                    Using Shortcut Menus

## OBJECTIVE                    **Estimated Time: 30 minutes**

• Use the shortcut menu to delete data

Last month you created a worksheet to keep track of your travel expenses. You would like to reuse the worksheet, but insert this month's expenses.

## INSTRUCTIONS

1. Create a new spreadsheet.

2. Key the data shown below as displayed.

3. Highlight cells B4 to E7.

4. Use the shortcuts to delete the data within the highlighted cells.

5. Enter the following data for this month's travel expenses:

|         | Week 1 | Week 2 | Week 3 | Week 4 |
|---------|--------|--------|--------|--------|
| Meals   | 48.20  | 84.76  | 95.00  | 48.39  |
| Car     | 35.78  | 87.34  | 56.90  | 88.50  |
| Lodging | 185.50 | 245.60 | 199.35 | 205.35 |
| Misc    | 24.56  | 43.19  | 16.28  | 48.99  |

6. Save the worksheet as ACT029.

7. Print the worksheet.

8. Close the file.

|   | A | B | C | D | E |
|---|---|---|---|---|---|
| 1 | Travel Expenses | | | | |
| 2 | | | | | |
| 3 | Rep | Week 1 | Week 2 | Week 3 | Week 4 |
| 4 | Meals | 44.98 | 65.61 | 72.01 | 31.05 |
| 5 | Car | 119.25 | 76.45 | 89.34 | 139.55 |
| 6 | Lodging | 212.20 | 177.75 | 154.53 | 199.87 |
| 7 | Misc | 37.05 | 65.45 | 89.19 | 33.34 |

# ACTIVITY 30　　　　　　　　　　　Formatting Numbers

## OBJECTIVE

**Estimated Time: 15 minutes**

• Use the dollar number format

　　You are comparative shopping between two grocery stores. You randomly take prices of several items in each store. You can then determine which store has, on average, the better prices.

## INSTRUCTIONS

1. Create a new spreadsheet.
2. Enter the data shown below.
3. Change the numbers format to the dollar format.
4. Save the spreadsheet as ACT030.
5. Print the spreadsheet.
6. Close the file.

|  | A | B | C |
|---|---|---|---|
| 1 |  | Store #1 | Store #2 |
| 2 | Celery | 1.35 | 1.33 |
| 3 | Milk | 2.56 | 2.59 |
| 4 | Bread | .99 | .99 |
| 5 | Eggs | .95 | .98 |
| 6 | Tom. Soup | .63 | .65 |
| 7 | Dish Soap | 2.39 | 2.45 |
| 8 | Tuna | 1.15 | .99 |
| 9 | O. Juice | 1.05 | .99 |
| 10 | P. Butter | 2.49 | 2.39 |
| 11 | Sand. Bags | 1.99 | 1.99 |
| 12 | Froz. Pizza | 2.99 | 2.95 |

# ACTIVITY 31

# Formatting Numbers

## OBJECTIVE

• Add commas to the number format

You are doing a report on the ecosystems of the world's largest deserts. You are keeping the information in a spreadsheet.

## INSTRUCTIONS

1. Create a new spreadsheet.

2. Enter the data shown below.

3. Change the number format to show commas in column C.

4. Save the spreadsheet as ACT031.

5. Print the spreadsheet.

6. Close the file.

| | A | B | C | D |
|---|---|---|---|---|
| 1 | The Largest Deserts | | | |
| 2 | Name | | Area (sq. mi.) | |
| 3 | Sahara | | 3500000 | |
| 4 | Gobi | | 500000 | |
| 5 | Great Victoria | | 250000 | |
| 6 | Gibson | | 250000 | |
| 7 | Rub'al-Khali | | 235000 | |
| 8 | Kalahari | | 225000 | |

# ACTIVITY 32

# Formatting Numbers

## OBJECTIVE

**Estimated Time: 10 minutes**

♦ Use the decimal number format

You are preparing a report for a driver's education class. In a spreadsheet, you have compiled a list of reasons for accidents.

## INSTRUCTIONS

1. Create a new spreadsheet.

2. Enter the data shown below.

3. Change the decimal places shown for all the numbers to two.

4. Save the spreadsheet as ACT032.

5. Print the spreadsheet.

6. Close the file.

| | A | B | C |
|---|---|---|---|
| 1 | Causes for Accidents | | |
| 2 | | | Percent |
| 3 | Speed | | 0.122 |
| 4 | Failed to yield | | 0.151 |
| 5 | Passed stop sign | | 0.02 |
| 6 | Disregarded signal | | 0.035 |
| 7 | Drove left of center | | 0.018 |
| 8 | Improper overtaking | | 0.013 |
| 9 | Made improper turn | | 0.045 |
| 10 | Followed too closely | | 0.055 |
| 11 | Other | | 0.227 |
| 12 | No apparent cause | | 0.314 |

# ACTIVITY 33                    Adding Borders and Lines

## OBJECTIVE                              **Estimated Time: 30 minutes**

• Add horizontal lines (borders) to enhance spreadsheet appearance

In order to make the appearance of your year-end report of Income and Expenses for each of your regional offices more readable you wish to add borders to separate the sections of the worksheet.

## INSTRUCTIONS

1. Create a new spreadsheet.

2. Key the data shown below.

3. Add a thick border to the bottom of A3 through E3.

4. Add a thick border to the bottom of A7 through E7.

5. Add a thick border to the bottom of A11 through E11.

6. Save the spreadsheet as ACT033.

7. Print the spreadsheet.

8. Close the file.

|    | A | B | C | D | E |
|----|---|---|---|---|---|
| 1 | Income and Expense Summary | | | | |
| 2 | (Number In Millions) | | | | |
| 3 | EAST | Q1 | Q2 | Q3 | Q4 |
| 4 | Income | 45 | 65 | 50 | 35 |
| 5 | Expenses | 40 | 42 | 49 | 41 |
| 6 | | | | | |
| 7 | MIDWEST | Q1 | Q2 | Q3 | Q4 |
| 8 | Income | 59 | 81 | 76 | 71 |
| 9 | Expenses | 60 | 72 | 66 | 45 |
| 10 | | | | | |
| 11 | WEST | Q1 | Q2 | Q3 | Q4 |
| 12 | Income | 98 | 87 | 76 | 89 |
| 13 | Expenses | 90 | 71 | 65 | 72 |

# ACTIVITY 34                    Adding Borders and Lines

## OBJECTIVE                    **Estimated Time: 15 minutes**

• Add lines (borders) to enhance the grid appearance of a table

Your price list contains discount column pricing for high volume purchases. You would like to enhance the appearance the Price List printout.

## INSTRUCTIONS

1. Create a new spreadsheet.

2. Key the data shown below.

3. Add a thick border to the bottom of A3 through E3.

4. Add a thin border to the left, right, top and bottom of A4 through E8.

5. Save the spreadsheet as ACT034.

6. Print the spreadsheet.

7. Close the file.

|   | A | B | C | D | E |
|---|---|---|---|---|---|
| 1 | PRICE LIST | | | | |
| 2 | | | | | |
| 3 | PRODUCT | QTY 1 | QTY 2 - 10 | QTY 11 - 20 | QTY 21+ |
| 4 | Widgets | 49.95 | 44.95 | 39.95 | 34.95 |
| 5 | Gadgets | 13.49 | 12.49 | 11.49 | 10.49 |
| 6 | Thingees | 29.95 | 27.95 | 25.95 | 23.95 |
| 7 | Gizmos | 8.95 | 7.95 | 6.95 | 5.95 |
| 8 | Doodads | 49.95 | 44.95 | 39.95 | 34.95 |

# ACTIVITY 35

# Aligning Data

## OBJECTIVE

**Estimated Time: 10 minutes**

• Right align column headings

You have noticed that the columns headings in a worksheet that tracks the wins and losses of the teams in your baseball league need to be right aligned.

## INSTRUCTIONS

1. Create a new spreadsheet.
2. Key the data shown below.
3. Right align the headings in B3 and C3.
4. Save the spreadsheet as ACT035.
5. Print the spreadsheet.
6. Close the file.

|   | A | B | C | D |
|---|---|---|---|---|
| 1 | League Standings | | | |
| 2 | | | | |
| 3 | Team | Wins | Losses | |
| 4 | Eagles | 22 | 6 | |
| 5 | Angels | 19 | 9 | |
| 6 | Tigers | 16 | 12 | |
| 7 | Gophers | 11 | 17 | |
| 8 | Gators | 9 | 19 | |

# ACTIVITY 36

# Aligning Data

## OBJECTIVE

**Estimated Time: 10 minutes**

• Center column headings

In a worksheet in which you have been tracking annual vacation and sick days for your employees, you think that the statistics would look better if they were centered.

## INSTRUCTIONS

1. Create a new spreadsheet.
2. Key the data shown below.
3. Center all of the data in cells B3 through C8.
4. Save the spreadsheet as ACT036.
5. Print the spreadsheet.
6. Close the file.

|   | A | B | C | D |
|---|---|---|---|---|
| 1 | Vacation & Sick Days | | | |
| 2 | | | | |
| 3 | Name | Vacation | Sick | |
| 4 | Gant | 5 | 4 | |
| 5 | Boone | 10 | 2 | |
| 6 | Davis | 3 | 3 | |
| 7 | Mayo | 0 | 0 | |
| 8 | Jacobs | 15 | 0 | |

# ACTIVITY 37

# Centering Text Across Columns

## OBJECTIVE

**Estimated Time: 10 minutes**

• Create and center a heading across several columns

You are to present the demographic study findings of your community to your store's manager. You want to make it more attractive by centering the category headings across the columns of data.

## INSTRUCTIONS

1. Open ACT010 that you created in Activity 10. If you did not complete Activity 10, key the data shown below.

2. Center the following headings across columns A through D: Population By Race, Population By Gender, Population Average Age, and Population Income.

3. Save the spreadsheet as ACT037.

4. Print the spreadsheet.

5. Close the file.

|    | A | B | C | D |
|----|---|---|---|---|
| 1  |   | 1980 | 1990 | 2000 |
| 2  | Population By Race | | | |
| 3  | White | 9,482 | 9,377 | 9,358 |
| 4  | Black | 8,259 | 9,386 | 10,015 |
| 5  | Hispanic | 3,566 | 5,612 | 6,836 |
| 6  | Asian | 1,997 | 3,743 | 4,474 |
| 7  | Population By Gender | | | |
| 8  | Female | 12,263 | 14,557 | 15,796 |
| 9  | Male | 11,041 | 13,561 | 14,887 |
| 10 | Population Average Age | | | |
| 11 |   | 33.5 | 33.0 | 33.4 |
| 12 | Population Income | | | |
| 13 | Average | 15,497 | 24,205 | 28,912 |
| 14 | Per Capita | 5,958 | 9,284 | 10,974 |

# ACTIVITY 38

# Entering Formulas

## OBJECTIVE

**Estimated Time: 15 minutes**

• Create an Autosum formula

You are a member of a volunteer fire department. You have a booth in a weeklong festival. From this booth, money is raised by selling T-shirts, hats, bumper stickers, and mugs that promote the fire department. You record the number of items sold each day in a spreadsheet.

## INSTRUCTIONS

1. Create a new spreadsheet.

2. Enter the data shown below.

3. In cell B7, use Autosum to total the range B2 through B5. This calculates the number of items sold on Monday.

4. Perform Autosum for Tuesday through Saturday in cells C7 through G7.

5. In cell H2, use Autosum to total the range B2 through G2. This calculates the number of T-shirts sold for the week.

6. Perform Autosum for hats, stickers, and mugs as well.

7. Save the spreadsheet as ACT038.

8. Print the spreadsheet.

9. Close the file.

|   | A | B | C | D | E | F | G | H |
|---|---|---|---|---|---|---|---|---|
| 1 |   | Mon | Tue | Wed | Thu | Fri | Sat | Total |
| 2 | T-shirts | 31 | 28 | 37 | 33 | 29 | 46 |   |
| 3 | Hats | 18 | 15 | 17 | 19 | 22 | 37 |   |
| 4 | Stickers | 14 | 9 | 11 | 6 | 10 | 19 |   |
| 5 | Mugs | 16 | 11 | 8 | 13 | 9 | 18 |   |
| 6 |   |   |   |   |   |   |   |   |
| 7 | Total |   |   |   |   |   |   |   |

# ACTIVITY 39

# Entering Formulas

## OBJECTIVES

* Create a subtraction formula
* Create a division formula

You have returned from a trip. You kept track of your odometer readings between fill-ups and the number of gallons each fill-up required. You use a spreadsheet to calculate the number of miles driven and the miles per gallon for your car.

## INSTRUCTIONS

1. Create a new spreadsheet.

2. Enter the data shown below.

3. In column C, enter the formula that calculates the number of miles driven for each stop.

4. In column E, enter the formula that calculates the miles per gallon (mileage divided by gallons).

5. Change number format in column E to display two decimal places.

6. Save the spreadsheet as ACT039.

7. Print the spreadsheet.

8. Close the file.

|    | A | B | C | D | E | F |
|----|-----------|--------|---------|---------|-----------------|---|
| 1  | Miles Per Gallon | | | | | |
| 2  | Beginning | Ending | Mileage | Gallons | Miles Per Gallon | |
| 3  | 32156 | 32345 | | 9.7 | | |
| 4  | 32345 | 32581 | | 11.9 | | |
| 5  | 32581 | 32798 | | 10.4 | | |
| 6  | 32798 | 33007 | | 10.3 | | |
| 7  | 33007 | 33216 | | 10.75 | | |
| 8  | 33216 | 33420 | | 10.2 | | |
| 9  | 33420 | 33653 | | 10.9 | | |
| 10 | 33653 | 33871 | | 11 | | |
| 11 | 33871 | 34074 | | 9.9 | | |

# ACTIVITY 40

# Entering Formulas

## OBJECTIVES

**Estimated Time: 20 minutes**

* Write a formula that sums a column of values
* Write a formula that calculates an average

You have been asked to calculate the student-to-teacher ratio in your local school district and to determine the total number of students and teachers in the district.

## INSTRUCTIONS

1. Create a new spreadsheet.

2. Key the data shown below.

3. In cell B9 write the following formula: +B4+B5+B6+B7.

4. In cell C9 write the following formula: +C4+C5+C6+C7.

5. In cell D4 write the formula to calculate the ratio of the number of students to the number of teachers at the kindergarten level. (Hint: Divide the number of students by the number of teachers.)

6. In cells D5 through D7 enter the formulas to calculate the student-to-teacher ratio for the other levels.

7. Save the spreadsheet as ACT040.

8. Print the spreadsheet.

9. Close the file.

|   | A | B | C | D | E |
|---|---|---|---|---|---|
| 1 | Student/Teacher Ratio | | | | |
| 2 | | | | | |
| 3 | Level | Students | Teachers | Ratio | |
| 4 | Kindergarten | 197 | 6 | | |
| 5 | Elementary | 437 | 13 | | |
| 6 | Middle | 515 | 20 | | |
| 7 | High | 399 | 25 | | |
| 8 | | | | | |
| 9 | Totals | | | | |

# ACTIVITY 41

Entering Formulas

## OBJECTIVES

- Write a formula that calculates the highest value in a range
- Write a formula that calculates the lowest value in a range

You are responsible for tracking the number of flight arrivals and departures at the local regional airport. Your supervisor wants to know the highest number of arrivals and departures and the lowest number of arrivals and departures over the course of a week.

## INSTRUCTIONS

1. Create a new spreadsheet.
2. Key the data shown below.
3. In cell B11 write the formula to calculate the largest number of arrivals for the week.
4. In cell C11 write the formula to calculate the largest number of departures for the week.
5. In cell B12 write the formula to calculate the smallest number of arrivals for the week.
6. In cell C12 write the formula to calculate the smallest number of departures for the week.
7. Save the spreadsheet as ACT041.
8. Print the spreadsheet.
9. Close the file.

|    | A          | B        | C          | D |
|----|------------|----------|------------|---|
| 1  | Arrivals & Departures | | | |
| 2  |            |          |            |   |
| 3  | Day        | Arrivals | Departures |   |
| 4  | Mon        | 124      | 114        |   |
| 5  | Tue        | 98       | 106        |   |
| 6  | Wed        | 154      | 130        |   |
| 7  | Thu        | 122      | 110        |   |
| 8  | Fri        | 187      | 221        |   |
| 9  | Sat        | 84       | 90         |   |
| 10 | Sun        | 216      | 185        |   |
| 11 | High       |          |            |   |
| 12 | Low        |          |            |   |

# ACTIVITY 42

# Changing Calculation Method

**OBJECTIVE**

**Estimated Time: 20 minutes**

♦ Set calculation mode to Manual

You have noticed that your large worksheet is taking a long time to update cells that contain formulas. In fact, it even takes longer to move from one cell to another after you have keyed in a new value. You have decided it would be better to have the worksheet calculate only when you ask it to.

## INSTRUCTIONS

1. Create a new spreadsheet.
2. Key the data shown below.
3. Set the calculation mode to Manual.
4. Enter formulas in cells D4 through D6 to calculate the total price of each order.
5. Change the value in B4 to **111.75**.
6. Change the value in B5 to **144.25**.
7. Observe that the results in D4 and D5 do not update.
8. Press the Calculation key to update the values in D4 and D5.
9. Save the spreadsheet as ACT042.
10. Print the spreadsheet.
11. Close the file.

|   | A | B | C | D |
|---|---|---|---|---|
| 1 | Order Record | | | |
| 2 | | | | |
| 3 | Order # | Amount | Shipping | Total |
| 4 | ABC-101 | 101.75 | 4.25 | |
| 5 | ABC-102 | 124.25 | 7.75 | |
| 6 | ABC-103 | 194.65 | 9.35 | |

# ACTIVITY 43

# Copying and Pasting

## OBJECTIVE

• Use the copy and paste commands

You are taking an ecology class. One of the requirements of the class is to study a zoological classification. You have chosen birds. You are to provide the geographic and ecologic regions of each species of bird. You record your findings in a spreadsheet.

## INSTRUCTIONS

1. Create a new spreadsheet.

2. Key the data shown on the next page through line 13.

3. Freeze titles so that the first 13 lines will always display on the screen.

4. Enter the names of the birds in column A beginning with line 14.

5. Since the titles are established, the abbreviations will always be seen.  Select the region abbreviations for each bird.  Copy the correct abbreviation and paste it in the appropriate cell. (For example, the Jackdaw's geographic region is Palearctic.  Copy PAL in A4 and paste it in C14.  The ecologic region is Mountains.  Copy the MOU in E8 and paste it in F14.)

6. Save the spreadsheet as ACT043.

7. Print the spreadsheet.

8. Close the file.

| | A | B | C | D | E | F | G | H |
|---|---|---|---|---|---|---|---|---|
| 1 | Geographic Classifications | | | | Ecologic Classifications | | | |
| 2 | Abrev. | Region | | | Abrev. | Region | | |
| 3 | ARC | Arctic | | | POL | Polar | | |
| 4 | PAL | Palearctic | | | TEM | Temperate & Coniferous | | |
| 5 | NEA | Nearctic | | | PRA | Prairies | | |
| 6 | ORI | Oriental | | | DES | Deserts | | |
| 7 | NEO | Neotropical | | | TRO | Tropical Forest | | |
| 8 | ETH | Ethiopian | | | MOU | Mountains | | |
| 9 | AUS | Australian | | | OCE | Oceans | | |
| 10 | ANT | Antarctic | | | CON | Continental Lakes and Rivers | | |
| 11 | WID | Widespread | | | WID | Widespread | | |
| 12 | | | | | | | | |
| 13 | Name | | Geographic Classifications | | | Ecologic Classifications | | |
| 14 | Jackdaw | | PAL | | | MOU | | |
| 15 | Goldfinch | | NEA | | | TEM | PRA | MOU |
| 16 | Wood Pigeon | | PAL | | | TEM | | |
| 17 | Rock Dove | | PAL | ORI | | TEM | PRA | MOU |
| 18 | Parrot | | ETH | | | TRO | | |
| 19 | Sandpiper | | WID | | | PRA | | |
| 20 | Pelican | | WID | | | CON | PRA | OCE |
| 21 | Peacock | | ORI | ETH | | TRO | | |
| 22 | Ortolan | | PAL | | | PRA | | |

# ACTIVITY 44

# Copying, Cutting, Pasting

## OBJECTIVE

**Estimated Time: 15 minutes**

◆ Use the cut, copy and paste commands

You are an NBA fan. You are keeping interesting statistics in a spreadsheet. One of the statistics you are keeping is the most all-time coaching victories. You will keep the name of the coach, number of wins and losses, and the winning percentage.

## INSTRUCTIONS

1. Create a new spreadsheet.

2. Enter the data shown below. Be sure to include the border under the column headings.

3. In cell E2 enter the formula, **=C2/(C2+D2)**. This formula computes the winning percentage. Format the cell to display three decimal places.

4. Copy the formula and paste it in the range for the other coaches' percentages.

5. You decide to add the headings:

   **Most All-Time Coaching Victories**

   **(Through the 1994 Season)**

   Cut the information entered in rows 1 through 12. Paste the information in the range beginning in cell A4. Then, enter the new headings (shown above) in rows 1 and 2. Center these headings across columns A through E.

6. Save the file as ACT044.

7. Print the spreadsheet.

8. Close the file.

|    | A | B | C | D | E |
|----|---|---|---|---|---|
| 1  | Coach | | Wins | Losses | Percent |
| 2  | Red Auerbach | | 938 | 479 | |
| 3  | Lenny Wilkens | | 926 | 774 | |
| 4  | Jack Ramsy | | 864 | 783 | |
| 5  | Dick Motta | | 856 | 863 | |
| 6  | Bill Fitch | | 845 | 877 | |
| 7  | Cotton Fitzsimmons | | 805 | 745 | |
| 8  | Don Nelson | | 803 | 573 | |
| 9  | Gene Shue | | 784 | 861 | |
| 10 | John MacLeod | | 707 | 657 | |
| 11 | Pat Riley | | 701 | 272 | |
| 12 | Red Holzman | | 696 | 604 | |

# ACTIVITY 45

# Drag and Drop

## OBJECTIVE

**Estimated Time: 10 minutes**

• Use the mouse to drag and drop data

You are starting a temporary-help business. You have little cash; therefore, you are looking for companies that will barter for your services. You have a list of things for which you need to barter.

## INSTRUCTIONS

1. Create a new spreadsheet.

2. Key the data shown below.

3. You want to separate the title from the list by two lines. Highlight the data in the list and using the mouse, drag and drop the list two lines below where it is now.

4. Save the spreadsheet as ACT045.

5. Print the spreadsheet.

6. Close the file.

|   | A | B | C |
|---|---|---|---|
| 1 | Things For Which I Need to Barter | | |
| 2 | Copier | | |
| 3 | Computer | | |
| 4 | Printer | | |
| 5 | Desk (2) | | |
| 6 | Chair | | |

# ACTIVITY 46

# Clearing Cells and Ranges

## OBJECTIVE

• Remove the data in a worksheet range

You would like to erase all of the values from the worksheet that you used to estimate the expenses for last year's trip to Hawaii so that you can estimate the cost for this year's trip to Fiji.

## INSTRUCTIONS

1. Create a new worksheet.
2. Key the data shown below. This is the information from the trip to Hawaii.
3. Clear all of the data in B4 through B8.
4. Save the spreadsheet as ACT046.
5. Print the spreadsheet.
6. Close the worksheet.

|    | A | B | C |
|----|---|---|---|
| 1  | Vacation Planner | | |
| 2  | | | |
| 3  | Item | Cost | |
| 4  | Flight | 747 | |
| 5  | Hotel | 950 | |
| 6  | Meals | 500 | |
| 7  | Car Rental | 350 | |
| 8  | Misc. | 1000 | |
| 9  | | | |
| 10 | Total | | |
| 11 | | | |

# ACTIVITY 47

# Using Cell Protection

## OBJECTIVE

**Estimated Time: 15 minutes**

+ Protect data in specific cells from being altered

You regularly find that you have accidentally overwritten cells that contain the names of your sales representatives. In order to keep this from happening, you decide to protect those cells.

## INSTRUCTIONS

1. Create a new spreadsheet.

2. Key the data shown below.

3. Protect cells A4 through A8 so that they may not be overwritten or erased.

4. Save the spreadsheet as ACT047.

5. Print the spreadsheet.

6. Close the file.

|    | A | B | C |
|----|-------------|-------|---|
| 1  | Sales Totals |       |   |
| 2  |             |       |   |
| 3  | Rep         | Sales |   |
| 4  | Morgan      |       |   |
| 5  | Nathan      |       |   |
| 6  | Brad        |       |   |
| 7  | Matt        |       |   |
| 8  | Jennifer    |       |   |
| 9  |             |       |   |
| 10 | Total       |       |   |

# ACTIVITY 48
# Using Cell Protection

## OBJECTIVE

**Estimated Time: 20 minutes**

• Protect formula cells from being overwritten or deleted

You have created a worksheet used by several people in your office. When entering data, some of your co-workers accidentally key data in cells containing formulas. Since the accuracy of the data is important to your supervisor, you decide to protect the cells that contain formulas.

## INSTRUCTIONS

1. Create a new spreadsheet.

2. Key the data shown below.

3. Enter formulas in cells B6 and C6 to determine the TV totals.

4. Enter formulas in cells B10 and C10 to determine the VCR totals.

5. Protect cells B6, C6, B10, and C10 so that they may not be overwritten or erased.

6. Save the spreadsheet as ACT048.

7. Print the spreadsheet.

8. Close the file.

| | A | B | C |
|---|---|---|---|
| 1 | Sales & Rentals | | |
| 2 | | Joe | Jane |
| 3 | TVs | | |
| 4 | Sales | 18 | 25 |
| 5 | Rentals | 41 | 65 |
| 6 | TV Totals | | |
| 7 | VCRs | | |
| 8 | Sales | 66 | 91 |
| 9 | Rentals | 38 | 55 |
| 10 | VCR Totals | | |

# ACTIVITY 49

# Copying Formats

## OBJECTIVE

**Estimated Time: 10 minutes**

• Copy a format from one cell to another

The high school marching band is selling candy to raise money for a trip to the state tournament in the spring. To encourage competition, the band director has divided the band into teams to see who can raise the most money. You are keeping the results on a spreadsheet.

## INSTRUCTIONS

1. Create a new spreadsheet.

2. Key the data shown below.

3. Format cell B2 to be a dollar format with no cents.

4. Copy that format to the other cells that need to show dollar amounts.

5. Save the spreadsheet as ACT049.

6. Print the spreadsheet.

7. Close the file.

|   | A | B | C | D | E |
|---|---|---|---|---|---|
| 1 | Team | Week 1 | Week 2 | Week 3 | Week 4 |
| 2 | Brass | 98 | 105 | 164 | 210 |
| 3 | Woodwind | 115 | 137 | 155 | 222 |
| 4 | Percussion | 76 | 89 | 145 | 165 |

# ACTIVITY 50

# Review

## OBJECTIVE

**Estimated Time: 75 minutes**

◆ Review the skills learned in Activities 15-49

You are setting up a family budget for the coming year. Your goal is to save enough money by next year to pay for a cruise for the entire family. By using a budget, you can forecast your income and expenses. Any amounts remaining after paying expenses will go to savings. Of the savings, 75 percent will go to general savings; the rest, towards your cruise.

## INSTRUCTIONS

1. Create a new spreadsheet.
2. Key the data shown on the next page. Notice that most of the budgeted items are the same for each month. Use copy and paste to save time inputting repeated figures.
3. Set horizontal and vertical titles so that the budget items and months will stay on the screen.
4. The following cells require the formulas described (In most cases, the formulas can be entered for January and then copied to the other months.):
   ◆ The Total cells for income and expenses are a sum of the appropriate range of cells.
   ◆ The Savings cells are a subtraction of the expenses Total cell from the income Total cell for each month.
   ◆ The General cells under Savings are a result of multiplying each Savings cell by 0.75.
   ◆ The Vacation cells under Savings are the subtraction of each General from each Savings cell.
   ◆ The Vacation Money result is a sum of the Vacation cells in row 27.
5. Make sure the following formats are included:
   ◆ "Household Budget" is centered across the column range A through M.
   ◆ The names of the months are centered in the cells.
   ◆ A thick border separates the month names from the data.
   ◆ The numbers are formatted for two decimal places.
   ◆ The totals have the dollar format with two decimal places.
6. Protect column A and rows 1 through 3.
7. Print the spreadsheet landscape. If possible, select the option to fit the printout on one page.
8. Preview the spreadsheet to see that it looks correct.
9. Print a range that shows the budget for January through March.
10. Save the spreadsheet as ACT050.
11. Close the file.

|   | A | B | C | D | E | F | G | H | I | J | K | L | M |
|---|---|---|---|---|---|---|---|---|---|---|---|---|---|
| 1 | | | | | | | Household Budget | | | | | | |
| 2 | | | | | | | | | | | | | |
| 3 | | Jan | Feb | Mar | Apr | May | Jun | Jul | Aug | Sep | Oct | Nov | Dec |
| 4 | Income | | | | | | | | | | | | |
| 5 | Husband | 1912.00 | 2006.00 | 2423.00 | 2201.00 | 2388.00 | 2571.00 | 2640.00 | 2549.00 | 2481.00 | 2407.00 | 2031.00 | 1985.00 |
| 6 | Wife | 2350.00 | 2350.00 | 2350.00 | 2350.00 | 2350.00 | 2350.00 | 2350.00 | 2350.00 | 2350.00 | 2350.00 | 2350.00 | 2350.00 |
| 7 | Interest | 56.21 | 57.90 | 59.63 | 61.42 | 63.26 | 65.16 | 67.11 | 69.13 | 71.20 | 73.34 | 75.54 | 77.80 |
| 8 | Dividends | | | 30.00 | | | 30.00 | | | 30.00 | | | 30.00 |
| 9 | Total | | | | | | | | | | | | |
| 10 | | | | | | | | | | | | | |
| 11 | Expenses | | | | | | | | | | | | |
| 12 | Car #1 | 267.00 | 267.00 | 267.00 | 267.00 | 267.00 | 267.00 | 267.00 | 267.00 | 267.00 | 267.00 | 267.00 | 267.00 |
| 13 | Car #2 | 219.25 | 219.25 | 219.25 | 219.25 | 219.25 | 219.25 | 219.25 | 219.25 | 219.25 | 219.25 | 219.25 | 219.25 |
| 14 | Car Ins. | 119.09 | 142.36 | 142.36 | 142.36 | 142.36 | 142.36 | 142.36 | 142.36 | 142.36 | 142.36 | 142.36 | 142.36 |
| 15 | Clothing | 100.00 | 100.00 | 100.00 | 100.00 | 100.00 | 100.00 | 100.00 | 100.00 | 100.00 | 100.00 | 100.00 | 100.00 |
| 16 | Entertain. | 150.00 | 150.00 | 150.00 | 150.00 | 150.00 | 150.00 | 150.00 | 150.00 | 150.00 | 150.00 | 150.00 | 150.00 |
| 17 | Food | 450.00 | 450.00 | 450.00 | 450.00 | 450.00 | 450.00 | 450.00 | 450.00 | 450.00 | 450.00 | 450.00 | 450.00 |
| 18 | Gas | 105.00 | 105.00 | 105.00 | 105.00 | 105.00 | 105.00 | 105.00 | 105.00 | 105.00 | 105.00 | 105.00 | 105.00 |
| 19 | Phone | 35.00 | 35.00 | 35.00 | 35.00 | 35.00 | 35.00 | 35.00 | 35.00 | 35.00 | 35.00 | 35.00 | 35.00 |
| 20 | Rent | 571.00 | 571.00 | 571.00 | 571.00 | 571.00 | 571.00 | 571.00 | 571.00 | 571.00 | 571.00 | 571.00 | 571.00 |
| 21 | Utilities | 105.00 | 105.00 | 105.00 | 105.00 | 105.00 | 105.00 | 105.00 | 105.00 | 105.00 | 105.00 | 105.00 | 105.00 |
| 22 | Misc. | 100.00 | 100.00 | 100.00 | 100.00 | 100.00 | 100.00 | 100.00 | 100.00 | 100.00 | 100.00 | 100.00 | 100.00 |
| 23 | Total | | | | | | | | | | | | |
| 24 | | | | | | | | | | | | | |
| 25 | Savings | | | | | | | | | | | | |
| 26 | General | | | | | | | | | | | | |
| 27 | Vacation | | | | | | | | | | | | |
| 28 | | | | | | | | | | | | | |
| 29 | Vacation Money | | | | | | | | | | | | |

# ACTIVITY 51                                    Create Your Own

## OBJECTIVES

- Create titles
- Format numbers
- Align data
- Add borders
- Enter formulas
- Copy and paste data
- Print a spreadsheet

You are comparative shopping for a new computer system. Decide on the system you want and shop at least three different places (computer stores or mail order companies) to see which gives you the best total price. You will need to decide things like how much RAM, disk storage, monitor size, kind of printer, etc. You will use a spreadsheet to make the calculations.

## INSTRUCTIONS

1. Create a new spreadsheet.

2. Use the example on the next page to set up your spreadsheet. You will use your own criteria; this is **only** an example. Since each store will have similar information, use copy and paste to duplicate similar information.

3. Perform the following formatting:

    - Center the heading across the columns.

    - Under each computer store name, put a solid border.

    - The cells with dollars should reflect the dollar format with no decimal places.

    - The word "Total:" is right aligned.

4. Do the necessary research for computer systems from at least three stores and input the data.

5. Save the spreadsheet as ACT051.

6. Print the spreadsheet.

7. Close the file.

|    | A | B | C | D | E |
|----|---|---|---|---|---|
| 1  | Comparison Shopping for Computers | | | | |
| 2  | | | | | |
| 3  | A to Z Computer Store | | | | Price |
| 4  | Super Fast Computer Brand | | | | $1,895 |
| 5  | | 8 Mg RAM | | | |
| 6  | | 540 Mg Drive | | | |
| 7  | | CD ROM Drive | | | |
| 8  | | Neat-oh! Speakers | | | |
| 9  | | | | | |
| 10 | Razor Sharp Laser Printer | | | | $995 |
| 11 | | | | | |
| 12 | Ditto Scanner | | | | $795 |
| 13 | | | | Total: | $3,685 |

# ACTIVITY 52                     Changing Column Widths

**OBJECTIVE**                              **Estimated Time:  10 minutes**

• Adjust column widths

  You are telling a friend about the NBA coaching statistics you are keeping. She would like a copy of those statistics. Before you print out the file, you notice that you can adjust column A to show the longest name, Cotton Fitzsimmons.

**INSTRUCTIONS**

1. Open ACT044 or key the data shown below. If you key the data, use the correct formula to calculate the winning percentages. (Hint: If you need help with the formula, refer to Activity 44.)

2. Adjust the width of column A so that Cotton Fitzsimmons fits.

3. Delete column B.

4. Save the spreadsheet as ACT052.

5. Print the spreadsheet.

6. Close the file.

| | A | B | C | D | E |
|---|---|---|---|---|---|
| 1 | Most All-Time Coaching Victories | | | | |
| 2 | (Through the 1994 Season) | | | | |
| 3 | | | | | |
| 4 | Coach | | Wins | Losses | Percent |
| 5 | Red Auerbach | | 938 | 479 | 0.662 |
| 6 | Lenny Wilkens | | 926 | 774 | 0.545 |
| 7 | Jack Ramsy | | 864 | 783 | 0.525 |
| 8 | Dick Motta | | 856 | 863 | 0.498 |
| 9 | Bill Fitch | | 845 | 877 | 0.491 |
| 10 | Cotton Fitzsimmons | | 805 | 745 | 0.519 |
| 11 | Don Nelson | | 803 | 573 | 0.584 |
| 12 | Gene Shue | | 784 | 861 | 0.477 |
| 13 | John MacLeod | | 707 | 657 | 0.518 |
| 14 | Pat Riley | | 701 | 272 | 0.720 |
| 15 | Red Holzman | | 696 | 604 | 0.535 |

# ACTIVITY 53

# Changing Column Widths

## OBJECTIVE

**Estimated Time: 15 minutes**

♦ Expand the width of worksheet columns

You are creating a worksheet that shows the distance of the planets from the Sun. Some of the numbers are too large to fit in the column. You will adjust the column width to display these numbers.

## INSTRUCTIONS

1. Create a new spreadsheet.

2. Key the data from the table shown below into columns A and B of the worksheet. Do not worry that some of the values that you enter in column B do not display properly.

The Planets

|         | Distance to the Sun (nearest million miles) |
|---------|---------------------------------------------|
| Mercury | 36000000                                    |
| Venus   | 67000000                                    |
| Earth   | 93000000                                    |
| Mars    | 141000000                                   |
| Jupiter | 484000000                                   |
| Saturn  | 888000000                                   |
| Uranus  | 1786000000                                  |
| Neptune | 2799000000                                  |
| Pluto   | 3666000000                                  |

3. Widen column B so that the label in B2 and the values in the column display fully within the column.

4. Format the values in B3 through B11 in comma format with no decimal places.

5. Save the worksheet as ACT053.

6. Print the spreadsheet.

7. Close the file.

# ACTIVITY 54

# Changing Text Sizes and Fonts

## OBJECTIVE

**Estimated Time: 10 minutes**

+ Change the font size and style

You want to print your worksheet for driver's education class and give it to your instructor. You decide to make the worksheet more attractive before printing it.

## INSTRUCTIONS

1. Load the file ACT032 or key the data shown below.
2. Change the heading, "Causes for Accidents," to bold, italic, 12 point.
3. Change "Percent" to bold.
4. Save the spreadsheet as ACT054.
5. Print the spreadsheet.
6. Close the file.

|    | A | B | C |
|----|---|---|---|
| 1  | Causes for Accidents | | |
| 2  | | | Percent |
| 3  | Speed | | 0.12 |
| 4  | Failed to yield | | 0.15 |
| 5  | Passed stop sign | | 0.02 |
| 6  | Disregarded signal | | 0.04 |
| 7  | Drove left of center | | 0.02 |
| 8  | Improper overtaking | | 0.01 |
| 9  | Made improper turn | | 0.05 |
| 10 | Followed too closely | | 0.06 |
| 11 | Other | | 0.23 |
| 12 | No apparent cause | | 0.31 |

# ACTIVITY 55

# Changing Text Size and Appearance

**OBJECTIVE**                                            **Estimated Time: 10 minutes**

* Change font size and style

After you create a worksheet showing the growth of the U.S. population over two centuries, you decide to enhance its appearance before printing it.

## INSTRUCTIONS

1. Create a new spreadsheet.

2. Key the data shown below.

3. Change the column widths to display the data attractively.

4. Change the style of title in cell A1 to bold, 16 point.

5. Change the column headings to bold, italic, 14 point.

6. Format the population figures for comma with zero decimal places.

7. Save the spreadsheet as ACT055.

8. Print the spreadsheet.

9. Close the file.

|   | A | B | C |
|---|---|---|---|
| 1 | U.S. Population Growth | | |
| 2 | | | |
| 3 | Year | Population | |
| 4 | 1790 | 3929214 | |
| 5 | 1890 | 62947714 | |
| 6 | 1990 | 248709873 | |

# ACTIVITY 56     Changing Text Appearance and Row Heights

## OBJECTIVES

**Estimated Time: 20 minutes**

• Change row heights
• Change font and style

    Your company has four departments. You create an employee directory listing last names, first names, departments, and phone extensions.

## INSTRUCTIONS

1. Create a new spreadsheet.

2. Enter the information shown on the next page.

3. Adjust column widths to display the data attractively.

4. To make the title stand out:

   • Change the font to Times, bold, 14 point. (If Times is not available, select another serif font.)

   • Increase the row height of row 1.

   • Center the title across the columns A through D.

   • Make the vertical alignment of the title centered.

5. Change the column heads to bold. Center the column heads.

6. Save the spreadsheet as ACT056.

7. Print the spreadsheet.

8. Close the file.

|  | A | B | C | D |
|---|---|---|---|---|
| 1 | Timely Investments Departmental List | | | |
| 2 | Last | First | Dept. | Exten. |
| 3 | Al-Haffar | Mohammad | AAM | 3345 |
| 4 | Andews | Janelle | TSE | 3367 |
| 5 | Baker | Dan | AAM | 3319 |
| 6 | Brown | Earl | AAM | 3378 |
| 7 | Burks | Michele | ITM | 3398 |
| 8 | Cobb | Mamie | JKU | 3318 |
| 9 | D'Aquila | Maria | TSE | 3366 |
| 10 | Fossett | Mack | ITM | 3307 |
| 11 | Goebel | Sara | AAM | 3396 |
| 12 | Gomez | Nigel | JKU | 3331 |
| 13 | Liu | Wang | JKU | 3375 |
| 14 | Loch | Lloyd | JKU | 3394 |
| 15 | Payne | Ima | ITM | 3311 |
| 16 | Polaski | Becky | JKU | 3372 |
| 17 | Ritter | Eugene | TSE | 3369 |
| 18 | Sawyer | Jan | ITM | 3373 |
| 19 | Snow | Keith | AAM | 3386 |
| 20 | Velasquez | Ana | TSE | 3354 |
| 21 | Workman | Nancy | TSE | 3327 |

# ACTIVITY 57                                    Removing Gridlines

## OBJECTIVE                          **Estimated Time:  10 minutes**

♦ Remove screen gridlines

## INSTRUCTIONS

1. Create a new spreadsheet.
2. Key the data shown below, applying bold and underline styles as depicted.
3. Turn off the worksheet gridlines.
4. Save the spreadsheet as ACT057.
5. Close the file.

|   | A | B | C | D |
|---|---|---|---|---|
| 1 | **Service Survey Results** | | | |
| 2 | | | | |
| 3 | **Rating** | **Males** | **Females** | |
| 4 | Excellent | 89 | 108 | |
| 5 | Good | 79 | 64 | |
| 6 | Average | 104 | 91 | |
| 7 | Poor | 55 | 39 | |

# ACTIVITY 58    Using Absolute and Relative References

**OBJECTIVE**                                                    **Estimated Time: 20 minutes**

• Use a formula that contains both a relative and an absolute reference

You are in charge of meal preparation for your family reunion. You still don't know how many people are coming; therefore, you cannot buy food until the day before. To date, the number of people attending is 17. Since you know that this number will change, you decide to create a spreadsheet to help you determine how much food to purchase.

## INSTRUCTIONS

1. Create a new spreadsheet.

2. Enter the data shown on the next page, applying the styles and formatting depicted.

3. In cell D6, enter the formula that multiplies B6 times C3. You will be copying this formula down the column so the reference to C3 will have to be absolute while the reference to B6 will be relative.

4. Copy this formula to cells D7 through D12 to determine how much of each item to buy.

5. Two days before the reunion Aunt Betty calls and conveys regrets that her family cannot attend. She has a family of 5. Change the number people attending from 17 to 12. Notice the changes in the amount of each food item to purchase.

6. Save the spreadsheet as ACT058.

7. Print the spreadsheet.

8. Close the file.

|    | A | B | C | D | E |
|----|---|---|---|---|---|
| 1  | **Food To Buy For Family Reunion** | | | | |
| 2  | | | | | |
| 3  | People Attending | | 17 | | |
| 4  | | | | | |
| 5  | Item | Amt./Person | Units | Amt. to Buy | |
| 6  | Turkey | 8 | ounces | | |
| 7  | Stuffing | 0.5 | cups | | |
| 8  | Corn | 0.3 | cups | | |
| 9  | Beans | 0.3 | cups | | |
| 10 | Rolls | 1.5 | each | | |
| 11 | Salad | 1.5 | cups | | |
| 12 | Pie | 1 | slice | | |

# ACTIVITY 59    Using Absolute and Relative References

## OBJECTIVE                                          Estimated Time: 20 minutes

• Write formulas containing relative and absolute references

The bonus paid to the sales representatives in your company is calculated as a percentage of each representative's total sales over a three month (quarterly) period. The bonus percentage varies with the quarter's profits.

## INSTRUCTIONS

1. Create a new spreadsheet.

2. Key the data shown on the next page.

3. In cell E4 enter the formula to sum David's sales for three months.

4. Copy this formula to cells E5 through E8.

5. Examine each cell from E4 through E8 and notice the way in which the formula has been copied.

6. In cell F4 enter the formula to calculate the David's bonus. The bonus rate must be entered as an absolute reference.

7. Copy this formula to cells F5 through F8.

8. Examine each cell from F4 through F8 and notice the way in which the formula has been copied.

9. Save the spreadsheet as ACT059.

10. Print the spreadsheet.

11. Close the file.

|   | A | B | C | D | E | F |
|---|---|---|---|---|---|---|
| 1 | Commissions | | | | Bonus Rate: | 10.0% |
| 2 | | | | | | |
| 3 | Rep | Jan | Feb | Mar | Totals | Bonus |
| 4 | David | 1925 | 2150 | 1850 | | |
| 5 | Kelly | 2450 | 2100 | 2050 | | |
| 6 | Kent | 2150 | 1750 | 2450 | | |
| 7 | Erron | 1425 | 1325 | 1975 | | |
| 8 | Darci | 2000 | 2275 | 2675 | | |

# ACTIVITY 60

# Using Mixed References

## OBJECTIVE

**Estimated Time: 20 minutes**

* Create a formula with a mixed reference

Mike and Sally are neighborhood kids who want to set up a refreshment stand just outside a local business two blocks from their home. They plan to earn extra money during the summer when the workers take breaks and lunch. They ask you to determine the selling price of each item assuming markups of 30 percent, 40 percent and 50 percent.

## INSTRUCTIONS

1. Create a new spreadsheet.

2. Key the data shown below as displayed.

3. Enter the following formula in cell B9 to calculate the selling price of lemonade with a 30% markup: **($B2*B$8)+$B2**. The formula includes mixed references to allow you to copy the formula both across and down to determine the remaining selling prices.

4. Copy the formula in cell B9 to the range B9 through D13. (When copying to a range, it is fine include the cell containing the formula being copied. In this case, B9 should be included in the range to which the formula is pasted.)

5. Save the spreadsheet as ACT060.

6. Print the spreadsheet so that Mike and Sally can see the results.

7. Close the file.

|    | A             | B      | C    | D    |
|----|---------------|--------|------|------|
| 1  | **Cost of Items** |        |      |      |
| 2  | Lemonade      | $0.33  |      |      |
| 3  | Fudge         | $0.17  |      |      |
| 4  | Chips         | $0.21  |      |      |
| 5  | Pop           | $0.25  |      |      |
| 6  | Candy         | $0.15  |      |      |
| 7  |               |        |      |      |
| 8  | **Selling Price** | 30%    | 40%  | 50%  |
| 9  | Lemonade      |        |      |      |
| 10 | Fudge         |        |      |      |
| 11 | Chips         |        |      |      |
| 12 | Pop           |        |      |      |
| 13 | Candy         |        |      |      |

# ACTIVITY 61

# Using @ Functions

## OBJECTIVES

+ Write a formula using the AVERAGE function
+ Write a formula using the MAX function
+ Write a formula using the MIN function

The semester has come to a close and you need to compute the averages of each student's total test scores.  You would also like statistics showing the highest, lowest, and average scores for each test.

## INSTRUCTIONS

1. Create a new spreadsheet.

2. Key the data shown on the following page.

3. In cell E4 write a formula containing a function to average Reta's three test scores.

4. Copy the formula in E4 to E5 through E9.

5. In cell B11 write a formula containing a function that will determine the highest (maximum) score for Test 1.

6. Copy the formula in B11 to C11 through E11.

7. In cell B12 write a formula containing a function that will determine the lowest (minimum) score for Test 1.

8. Copy the formula in B12 to C12 through E12.

9. In cell B13 write a formula containing a function that will determine the average score for Test 1.

10. Copy the formula in B13 to C13 through E13.

11. Format the averages for zero decimal places.

12. Save the spreadsheet as ACT061.

13. Print the spreadsheet.

14. Close the file.

|    | A                 | B      | C      | D      | E    |
|----|-------------------|--------|--------|--------|------|
| 1  | Test Score Results |        |        |        |      |
| 2  |                   |        |        |        |      |
| 3  | Student           | Test 1 | Test 2 | Test 3 | Avg. |
| 4  | Reta              | 94     | 100    | 70     |      |
| 5  | Paige             | 76     | 72     | 72     |      |
| 6  | Bill              | 82     | 70     | 96     |      |
| 7  | Angie             | 78     | 90     | 72     |      |
| 8  | Jeff              | 96     | 74     | 90     |      |
| 9  | Gail              | 66     | 72     | 70     |      |
| 10 |                   |        |        |        |      |
| 11 | High              |        |        |        |      |
| 12 | Low               |        |        |        |      |
| 13 | Average           |        |        |        |      |

# ACTIVITY 62

# Using @ Functions

## OBJECTIVES

**Estimated Time: 10 minutes**

+ Use the TODAY function
+ Use the SUM function

You own a small lawn service called **New Leaf Lawn Care**. You want to create an invoice system using your spreadsheet software. You will create a template that can be used to prepare each invoice.

## INSTRUCTIONS

1. Create a new spreadsheet.

2. Key the data shown on the next page. Use the formatting displayed for text, alignment, and borders.

3. Every time you open the invoice file, you want it to display today's date. Enter the function that displays the current date in cell D4.

4. In cell D17, enter the formula to sum the range D7 through D16.

5. Print the spreadsheet.

6. Save the spreadsheet as ACT062.

7. Close the file.

|    | A | B | C | D |
|----|---|---|---|---|
| 1  | **Invoice** | | | |
| 2  | New Leaf Lawn Care | | | |
| 3  | | | | |
| 4  | | | Date: | |
| 5  | | | | |
| 6  | Description | | | Amount |
| 7  | | | | |
| 8  | | | | |
| 9  | | | | |
| 10 | | | | |
| 11 | | | | |
| 12 | | | | |
| 13 | | | | |
| 14 | | | | |
| 15 | | | | |
| 16 | | | | |
| 17 | | | Total: | |
| 18 | | | | |

# ACTIVITY 63

# Using @ Functions

## OBJECTIVE

**Estimated Time: 20 minutes**

◆ Write a formula using the COUNT function

You are conducting a brief survey of your customers.  The three possible responses to the question are Yes, No, and Unsure.  You set up a worksheet to count the number of Yes, No, and Unsure responses.

## INSTRUCTIONS

1. Create a new spreadsheet.

2. Key the data shown below.

3. In cell B12 enter a formula containing a function that will count all of the "X's" in range B5 through B10.

4. Copy the formula in B12 to C12 through D12.

5. Save the spreadsheet as ACT063.

6. Print the spreadsheet.

7. Close the file.

|  | A | B | C | D | E |
|---|---|---|---|---|---|
| 1 | Customer Survey | | | | |
| 2 | Question: Would you visit us again? | | | | |
| 3 | | | | | |
| 4 | | Yes | No | Unsure | |
| 5 | Customer 1 | X | | | |
| 6 | Customer 2 | X | | | |
| 7 | Customer 3 | | | X | |
| 8 | Customer 4 | | X | | |
| 9 | Customer 5 | X | | | |
| 10 | Customer 6 | | X | | |
| 11 | | | | | |
| 12 | Count | | | | |

# ACTIVITY 64

## OBJECTIVE

**Estimated Time: 15 minutes**

+ Use the PAYMENT function

You are getting ready to buy a car. You are comparing several cars. You want to use the spreadsheet to calculate your monthly payment depending on car cost and interest rate.

## INSTRUCTIONS

1. Create a new spreadsheet.

2. Key the data shown below as displayed.

3. In cell C5, use the payment function to determine the monthly payment. The number format should be dollar with zero decimal places.

4. Change the interest rate to 7.5% and notice the change in payment.

5. Change the cost of car to $9,000 and notice the change of payment.

6. Print the spreadsheet.

7. Save the spreadsheet as ACT064.

8. Close the file.

|   | A | B | C |
|---|---|---|---|
| 1 | Cost of Car | | $11,000 |
| 2 | Interest Rate | | 9.00% |
| 3 | No. of Payments | | 48 |
| 4 | | | |
| 5 | Payment | | |

# ACTIVITY 65

# Copying the Results of a Formula

## OBJECTIVE

**Estimated Time: 20 minutes**

* Copy the results from cells that contain formulas

You would like to keep the final averages of your skating team members to use for future comparisons.

## INSTRUCTIONS

1. Create a new spreadsheet.
2. Key the data shown below.
3. In cell E4 enter a formula that will average each skater's scores.
4. Copy the formula in E4 to cells E5 through E7.
5. Format cells E4 through E7 for one decimal place.
6. Copy the results of the formulas in cells E4 through E7 to cells F4 through F7.
7. Save the spreadsheet as ACT065.
8. Print the spreadsheet.
9. Close the file.

|   | A | B | C | D | E | F |
|---|---|---|---|---|---|---|
| 1 | Skating Team Averages | | | | | |
| 2 | | | | | | |
| 3 | Skater | Score 1 | Score 2 | Score 3 | Avg. Score | Last Year |
| 4 | Brad | 8.3 | 8.7 | 8.9 | | |
| 5 | Laura | 9.1 | 9.5 | 8.7 | | |
| 6 | Amanda | 9.5 | 9.6 | 9.3 | | |
| 7 | Stephanie | 9.9 | 9.8 | 9.9 | | |
| 8 | | | | | | |
| 9 | | | | | | |

# ACTIVITY 66                     Viewing a List of Functions

**OBJECTIVE**                                    **Estimated Time: 10 minutes**

• Access a list of functions

    Next week you will be starting a new job. In that position, you will be required to perform financial and statistical analyses with a spreadsheet. You want to review the different kinds of functions in each category.

**INSTRUCTIONS**

1. Create a new spreadsheet.
2. View the list of financial functions.
3. View the list of statistical functions.
4. Close the file without saving.

# ACTIVITY 67    Adding @ Function to Pull-Down Menu

## OBJECTIVES

**Estimated Time:  10 minutes**

- Add the MAX function to the @Function List
- Add the MIN function to the @Function List

You use the MAX and MIN functions frequently; therefore, you decide to add these functions to the list of other functions that are on the pull-down function menu.

## INSTRUCTIONS

1. Create a new spreadsheet.

2. Add the MAX function to the Functions pull-down menu (list).

3. Add the MIN function to the Functions pull-down menu (list).

4. Close the spreadsheet without saving.

# ACTIVITY 68

# Creating and Using Charts

## OBJECTIVE

**Estimated Time: 15 minutes**

* Create a pie chart

You are researching the continents. You have prepared a list of the continents and the area in square miles for each continent.

## INSTRUCTIONS

1. Create a new spreadsheet.
2. Key the data shown below as displayed. Adjust column widths as necessary.
3. Create a pie chart with the continent names as labels.
4. Save the spreadsheet and chart as ACT068.
5. Print the pie chart.
6. Close the chart and spreadsheet.

|   | A | B |
|---|---|---|
| 1 | **Continent** | **Area** |
| 2 | Africa | 11,678,000 |
| 3 | Antarctica | 5,400,000 |
| 4 | Asia | 17,005,000 |
| 5 | Australia | 2,967,900 |
| 6 | Europe | 4,069,000 |
| 7 | North America | 9,351,000 |
| 8 | South America | 6,885,000 |

# ACTIVITY 69

# Creating and Using Charts

## OBJECTIVES

**Estimated Time: 15 minutes**

* Create a pie chart
* Add a title to a chart

You asked a random group of customers which flavor of ice cream they prefer. You will create a pie chart showing the results.

## INSTRUCTIONS

1. Create a new spreadsheet.

2. Key the data shown below.

3. Create a pie chart from the range A3 through B8.

4. Add the following title to your chart: **Flavor Preferences**

5. Save the spreadsheet and chart as ACT069.

6. Print the chart.

7. Close the chart and spreadsheet.

|   | A | B | C |
|---|---|---|---|
| 1 | Ice Cream Survey | | |
| 2 | | | |
| 3 | Flavor | Number | |
| 4 | Vanilla | 38 | |
| 5 | Chocolate | 22 | |
| 6 | Strawberry | 15 | |
| 7 | Peppermint | 10 | |
| 8 | Rocky Road | 5 | |

# ACTIVITY 70

# Changing Chart Types

## OBJECTIVE

**Estimated Time: 15 minutes**

• Change from one chart type to another

You are doing research on the increase of pollution in the world. You have found statistics for the countries that produce the most garbage per person per year.

## INSTRUCTIONS

1. Create a new spreadsheet.

2. Key the data shown below.

3. Create a pie chart without labels.

4. Change the pie chart to a horizontal bar chart.

5. Save the spreadsheet and chart as ACT070.

6. Print the bar chart.

7. Close the chart and spreadsheet.

| | A | B | C | D | E |
|---|---|---|---|---|---|
| 1 | Country | Pounds per person per annum | | | |
| 2 | U.S. | 1,905 | | | |
| 3 | Canada | 1,378 | | | |
| 4 | Finland | 1,111 | | | |
| 5 | Norway | 1,043 | | | |
| 6 | Denmark | 1,034 | | | |

# ACTIVITY 71

# Changing Chart Types

## OBJECTIVE

**Estimated Time: 15 minutes**

• Change from one chart type to another

You are planning a camping trip to Europe next summer. As you are making your plans, you decide to research the average rainfall of several cities to see which has the least rain during the summer months and which month might be the best one for travel.

## INSTRUCTIONS

1. Create a new spreadsheet.

2. Key the data shown below.

3. Create a bar chart from the data.

4. You notice that the bar chart is hard to read so create a line chart with data points. Use the Y-axis for the amount of rainfall and the X-axis for the months. Each city will be represented by a different line.

5. Use a legend to make the chart easier to understand.

6. Set the Y-axis for a minimum value of 0 and a maximum value of 90.

7. Print the spreadsheet.

8. Save the spreadsheet as ACT071.

9. Close the file.

|   | A | B | C | D | E | F |
|---|---|---|---|---|---|---|
| 1 | Average Rainfall of European Cities (In Millimeters) | | | | | |
| 2 |   | May | Jun | Jul | Aug | Sep |
| 3 | Athens | 15 | 5 | 5 | 5 | 15 |
| 4 | Berlin | 60 | 70 | 80 | 70 | 50 |
| 5 | London | 45 | 50 | 40 | 50 | 55 |
| 6 | Paris | 50 | 50 | 55 | 60 | 50 |
| 7 | Rome | 35 | 20 | 5 | 35 | 75 |

# ACTIVITY 72

# Changing Chart Types

## OBJECTIVE

**Estimated Time: 10 minutes**

• Change from one chart type to another

You have started taking an art class. Just for fun you research artists who had the most paintings sold for over $1,000,000.

## INSTRUCTIONS

1. Create a new spreadsheet.

2. Key the data shown below.

3. Create a pie chart with a legend.

4. Change the chart to a vertical bar chart without a legend.

5. Save the spreadsheet and chart as ACT072.

6. Print the vertical bar chart.

7. Close the chart and spreadsheet.

|    | A | B | C |
|----|---|---|---|
| 1 | Artist | No. Sold Over $1M | |
| 2 | Pablo Picasso | 148 | |
| 3 | Pierre-Auguste Renoir | 142 | |
| 4 | Claude Monet | 126 | |
| 5 | Edgar Degas | 64 | |
| 6 | Marc Chagall | 53 | |
| 7 | Camille Pissarro | 49 | |
| 8 | Henri Matisse | 45 | |
| 9 | Paul Cezanne | 42 | |
| 10 | Vincent van Gogh | 32 | |

# ACTIVITY 73

Adding Titles to a Chart

## OBJECTIVE

Estimated Time: 15 minutes

• Add a title to an existing chart

Your friend works for a travel agency and likes the chart you created for the average rainfall for selected European cities. Your friend asks for a copy of the chart, but would like it to include a title.

## INSTRUCTIONS

1. Open ACT071, including the chart. If you did not complete Activity 71, key the data shown below and create a line chart that includes data points. Use the Y-axis for the amount of rainfall and the X-axis for the months. Each city will be represented by a different line. Include a legend. Set the Y-axis for a minimum value of 0 and a maximum value of 90.

2. Key in the following for a title:

**Average Rainfall of European Cities**

**(In Millimeters)**

3. Print the chart.

4. Save the chart and the spreadsheet as ACT073.

5. Close the file.

|   | A | B | C | D | E | F |
|---|---|---|---|---|---|---|
| 1 | Average Rainfall of European Cities (In Millimeters) | | | | | |
| 2 |   | May | Jun | Jul | Aug | Sep |
| 3 | Athens | 15 | 5 | 5 | 5 | 15 |
| 4 | Berlin | 60 | 70 | 80 | 70 | 50 |
| 5 | London | 45 | 50 | 40 | 50 | 55 |
| 6 | Paris | 50 | 50 | 55 | 60 | 50 |
| 7 | Rome | 35 | 20 | 5 | 35 | 75 |

# ACTIVITY 74     Adding Axis Descriptions to a Chart

## OBJECTIVE

**Estimated Time: 10 minutes**

* Use a description on a chart axis

    You decide to add axis descriptions to the chart on world pollution statistics.

## INSTRUCTIONS

1.  Load ACT070 including the chart, or key the data shown below.

2.  Create a vertical bar chart, if necessary.

3.  Add the title, **Country**, to the Y axis.

4.  Add the title, **Pounds Per Person**, to the X axis.

5.  Save the spreadsheet and chart as ACT074.

6.  Print the chart.

7.  Close the chart and spreadsheet.

|   | A | B | C | D | E |
|---|---|---|---|---|---|
| 1 | Country | Pounds per person per annum | | | |
| 2 | U.S. | 1,905 | | | |
| 3 | Canada | 1,378 | | | |
| 4 | Finland | 1,111 | | | |
| 5 | Norway | 1,043 | | | |
| 6 | Denmark | 1,034 | | | |

# ACTIVITY 75                    Adding Features to a Chart

**OBJECTIVES**                    **Estimated Time:  25 minutes**

+ Add data labels to a chart
+ Change the fill of bars to a hatched pattern
+ Insert gridlines

You have just opened a new store and want to monitor the volume of traffic throughout the day. This will help you schedule your floor and register help for the peak times. You will count the number of people who enter the store during 15 minute periods at certain times in the day.

## INSTRUCTIONS

1. Key the data shown below.

2. Create a bar chart diagramming the traffic volume. Use the Y-axis to display the number of people and the X-axis to display the times of day.

3. Add data labels explaining the Y-axis data.

4. The color bars look fine on the monitor. However, you will only be able to print the chart on a non-color printer. You decide to change the fill of the bars from a color to a hatch pattern so the printout will be easier to read.

5. Add a Y-axis title that reads, **Number of People in 15 Minutes**.

6. Add an X-axis title that reads, **Time Count Ended**.

7. Add gridlines to the Y-axis. The gridlines should appear in 5 person increments.

8. Print the chart.

9. Save the chart and spreadsheet as ACT075.

10. Close the chart and the spreadsheet.

|   | A | B | C |
|---|---|---|---|
| 1 | Time | # of People | |
| 2 | 10:30 | 13 | |
| 3 | 12:30 | 27 | |
| 4 | 2:30 | 9 | |
| 5 | 5:30 | 27 | |
| 6 | 7:30 | 36 | |

# ACTIVITY 76

# Creating and Using Databases

## OBJECTIVES

**Estimated Time: 30 minutes**

• Create a database
• Find records meeting specific criteria

You are researching universities that you would like to attend. One of the criteria is the quality of the libraries. You record the data in a spreadsheet so that you can access the information more readily.

## INSTRUCTIONS

1. Create a new spreadsheet.

2. Key the data shown below. Make the field titles in row 1 bold.

3. From the Location field, find all the records of schools that are located in California.

4. Save the spreadsheet as ACT076.

5. Print the database.

6. Close the file.

|    | A | B | C |
|----|---|---|---|
| 1  | **Library** | **Location** | **# of Books** |
| 2  | Harvard University | Cambridge, Massachusetts | 12,394,894 |
| 3  | Yale University | New Haven, Connecticut | 9,173,981 |
| 4  | University of Illinois | Urbana, Illinois | 8,096,040 |
| 5  | University of California | Berkeley, California | 7,854,630 |
| 6  | University of Texas | Austin, Texas | 6,680,406 |
| 7  | University of Michigan | Ann Arbor, Michigan | 6,598,574 |
| 8  | Columbia University | New York, New York | 6,262,162 |
| 9  | University of California | Los Angeles, California | 6,247,320 |
| 10 | Stanford Univesity | Stanford, California | 6,127,388 |
| 11 | Cornell University | Ithaca, New York | 5,468,870 |

# ACTIVITY 77                                         Creating and Using Databases

## OBJECTIVES                                          **Estimated Time: 20 minutes**

+ Create a database
+ Find records meeting specific criteria

You are taking a class in sociology and are researching public transportation. As a part of your research, you are building a database of cities with underground railway systems. The database includes such facts as the year each system was begun, the total length of each system, the number of lines currently existing in each system, and the number of stations used by each system.

## INSTRUCTIONS

1. Create a new spreadsheet.

2. Key the data shown on the next page.

3. Using the database functions of your spreadsheet, find those cities that have 10 lines or more.

4. Print the results, if possible.

5. Save the spreadsheet as ACT077.

6. Close the file.

|  | A | B | C | D | E |
|---|---|---|---|---|---|
| 1 | **Major Cities With Underground Railways** | | | | |
| 2 | | | | | |
| 3 | City | Year Begun | Total Length | No. of Lines | No. of Stations |
| 4 | | | (miles) | | |
| 5 | London | 1863 | 245 | 10 | 273 |
| 6 | New York | 1868 | 232 | 23 | 466 |
| 7 | Paris | 1900 | 191 | 18 | 430 |
| 8 | Moscow | 1935 | 140 | 8 | 123 |
| 9 | Tokyo | 1927 | 135 | 10 | 192 |
| 10 | Berlin | 1902 | 104 | 8 | 134 |
| 11 | Chicago | 1892 | 97 | 6 | 142 |
| 12 | Copenhagen | 1934 | 84 | 7 | 61 |
| 13 | Mexico City | 1969 | 78 | 5 | 57 |
| 14 | Washington D.C. | 1976 | 73 | 3 | 47 |
| 15 | Seoul | 1974 | 72 | 2 | 20 |
| 16 | San Francisco | 1972 | 71 | 1 | 34 |
| 17 | Madrid | 1919 | 70 | 11 | 141 |
| 18 | Stockholm | 1950 | 67 | 3 | 94 |
| 19 | Osaka | 1933 | 57 | 6 | 88 |

# ACTIVITY 78

# Creating a Number Series

## OBJECTIVE

**Estimated Time: 15 minutes**

+ Create a number series in a column

You are taking a course in world geography. You create a spreadsheet showing population of various countries. By using the database features of the spreadsheet, you can sort and find information.

## INSTRUCTIONS

1. Create a new spreadsheet.
2. Key the data shown below as displayed.
3. In the Rank column create a sequential number series starting with 1.
4. Save the spreadsheet as ACT078.
5. Print the spreadsheet.
6. Close the file.

|   | A | B | C |
|---|---|---|---|
| 1 | **Population in Year 2000** | | |
| 2 | **Rank** | **Country** | **Population** |
| 3 | | China | 1,260,154,000 |
| 4 | | India | 1,018,105,000 |
| 5 | | U.S. | 275,327,000 |
| 6 | | Indonesia | 219,496,000 |
| 7 | | Brazil | 169,543,000 |
| 8 | | Russia | 151,460,000 |
| 9 | | Pakistan | 148,540,000 |
| 10 | | Bangladesh | 143,548,000 |
| 11 | | Japan | 127,554,000 |
| 12 | | Nigeria | 118,620,000 |

# ACTIVITY 79

# Setting Start and Increment Values

## OBJECTIVES

Estimated Time: 30 minutes

- Create a database
- Create a list of incremental values

You are a member of a golf league. You want to impress your partners with golf trivia. You create a database using your spreadsheet to list the winners of major golf tournaments. You begin your database by listing the winners of the U.S. Open from 1970 through 1990.

## INSTRUCTIONS

1. Create a new spreadsheet.
2. Type **Tournament Winners** in cell A1.
3. Type **Year, Winner, Event** and **Score** for field titles in cells A2 through D2.
4. Instead of keying each year, set the starting number as 1970, and, in increments of 1, fill down the column through 1990.
5. Key the rest of the data shown on the next page. Since this is information for the U.S. Open, use the fill down feature for this column.
6. Print the spreadsheet.
7. Save the spreadsheet as ACT079.
8. Close the file.

|   | A | B | C | D |
|---|---|---|---|---|
| 1 | **Tournament Winners** | | | |
| 2 | Year | Winner | Event | Score |
| 3 | 1970 | Tony Jacklin | U.S. Open | 281 |
| 4 | 1971 | Lee Trevino | U.S. Open | 280 |
| 5 | 1972 | Jack Nicklaus | U.S. Open | 290 |
| 6 | 1973 | Johnny Miller | U.S. Open | 279 |
| 7 | 1974 | Hale Irwin | U.S. Open | 287 |
| 8 | 1975 | Lou Graham | U.S. Open | 287 |
| 9 | 1976 | Jerry Pate | U.S. Open | 277 |
| 10 | 1977 | Hubert Green | U.S. Open | 278 |
| 11 | 1978 | Andy North | U.S. Open | 285 |
| 12 | 1979 | Hale Irwin | U.S. Open | 284 |
| 13 | 1980 | Jack Nicklaus | U.S. Open | 272 |
| 14 | 1981 | David Graham | U.S. Open | 273 |
| 15 | 1982 | Tom Watson | U.S. Open | 282 |
| 16 | 1983 | Larry Nelson | U.S. Open | 280 |
| 17 | 1984 | Fuzzy Zoeller | U.S. Open | 276 |
| 18 | 1985 | Andy North | U.S. Open | 279 |
| 19 | 1986 | Raymond Floyd | U.S. Open | 279 |
| 20 | 1987 | Scott Simpson | U.S. Open | 277 |
| 21 | 1988 | Curtis Strange | U.S. Open | 278 |
| 22 | 1989 | Curtis Strange | U.S. Open | 278 |
| 23 | 1990 | Hale Irwin | U.S. Open | 280 |

# ACTIVITY 80

# Sorting a Database

## OBJECTIVE

**Estimated Time: 15 minutes**

• Sort information numerically and alphabetically

For chemistry class, you are creating a database in your spreadsheet to record melting and boiling points for different elements.

## INSTRUCTIONS

1. Create a new spreadsheet.
2. Key the data shown below.
3. Sort the database in ascending order by melting point.
4. Sort the database in ascending order by boiling point.
5. Sort the database to alphabetize the elements.
6. Save the spreadsheet as ACT080.
7. Print the spreadsheet.
8. Close the file.

|    | A | B | C |
|----|----------|---------------|---------------|
| 1  | **Element** | **Melting Point** | **Boiling Point** |
| 2  | Aluminum | 1220 | 4473 |
| 3  | Calcium | 1542 | 2703 |
| 4  | Copper | 1981 | 4653 |
| 5  | Gold | 1947 | 5086 |
| 6  | Hydrogen | -434 | -423 |
| 7  | Iron | 2795 | 4982 |
| 8  | Mercury | -38 | 675 |
| 9  | Nickel | 2647 | 4950 |
| 10 | Nitrogen | -346 | -321 |
| 11 | Oxygen | -360 | -297 |
| 12 | Silver | 1764 | 4014 |
| 13 | Tin | 450 | 4118 |
| 14 | Uranium | 2070 | 6904 |

# ACTIVITY 81

# Sorting a Database

## OBJECTIVE

**Estimated Time: 30 minutes**

• Sort information in a spreadsheet both numerically and alphabetically

A local university is having international awareness week. The goal of the week is to become better acquainted with the lifestyles of people all over the world. The public is being invited to attend the activities. The sponsors of the events have asked everyone who attends to bring some information that will expand the awareness of the lifestyles of people in other countries. Since cars are your hobby, you decide to bring a list of people per car for several countries.

## INSTRUCTIONS

1. Create a new spreadsheet.

2. Key the data shown on the next page.

3. Sort the list in descending order by Person per Car.

4. Print the sorted list.

5. Now sort the list alphabetically.

6. Print the alphabetic listing.

7. Save the spreadsheet as ACT081.

8. Close the file.

|   | A | B | C |
|---|---|---|---|
| 1 | Country | People Per Car | |
| 2 | Germany | 2.5 | |
| 3 | Brazil | 13.5 | |
| 4 | Japan | 4.1 | |
| 5 | Poland | 10.2 | |
| 6 | Sweden | 2.5 | |
| 7 | USA | 1.7 | |
| 8 | Canada | 2.2 | |
| 9 | United Kingdom | 2.7 | |
| 10 | Mexico | 15 | |
| 11 | Switzerland | 2.3 | |
| 12 | India | 500 | |
| 13 | Ireland | 4.8 | |
| 14 | South Africa | 10.5 | |
| 15 | Argentina | 7.9 | |
| 16 | Spain | 4 | |
| 17 | Turkey | 45.3 | |
| 18 | Saudi Arabia | 8.7 | |
| 19 | France | 2.5 | |
| 20 | Italy | 2.5 | |
| 21 | Russia | 24 | |
| 22 | Australia | 2.2 | |

# ACTIVITY 82

Creating a Query Table

## OBJECTIVE

**Estimated Time: 20 minutes**

* Select information from a database using a query table

You are doing a report on great women of the twentieth century. One section of your report is on women who won a Nobel Prize. You have just started your research; therefore, the list is not complete.

## INSTRUCTIONS

1. Create a new spreadsheet.
2. Key the data shown below as displayed.
3. Create a query that lists the women who won the prize in literature.
4. Print that list.
5. Save the spreadsheet as ACT082.
6. Close the file.

|    | A | B | C | D |
|----|----------|-----------|------------|------|
| 1  | **Winner** | **Nationality** | **Prize** | **Year** |
| 2  | Marie Curie | Polish | Physics | 1903 |
| 3  | Bertha von Suttner | Austrian | Peace | 1905 |
| 4  | Selma Lagerlof | Swedish | Literature | 1909 |
| 5  | Marie Curie | Polish | Chemistry | 1911 |
| 6  | Grazia Deledda | Italian | Literature | 1926 |
| 7  | Sigrid Undset | Norwegian | Literature | 1928 |
| 8  | Jane Addams | American | Peace | 1931 |
| 9  | Irene Joliot-Curie | French | Chemistry | 1935 |
| 10 | Pearl Buck | American | Literature | 1938 |
| 11 | Gabriela Mistral | Chilean | Literature | 1945 |

# ACTIVITY 83          Creating and Using a Query Table

## OBJECTIVES                                    **Estimated Time: 30 minutes**

- Extract data into a query table
- Specify query criterion

You are in charge of the aerobics division of the Creative Fitness Center. You need to create a list of all members who have asked to be notified when the new Walkercize aerobics classes begin.

## INSTRUCTIONS

1. Create a new spreadsheet.

2. Key the data shown below as displayed.

3. Set up an extract block at a convenient location within the spreadsheet.

4. Extract the **Name** and **Phone** of all of the members are interested in Walkercize.

5. Print the list you extracted.

6. Save the spreadsheet as ACT083.

7. Close the spreadsheet.

|    | A | B | C | D |
|----|---|---|---|---|
| 1  | Aerobics Notification List | | | |
| 2  | | | | |
| 3  | Name | Phone | Interest | |
| 4  | Huntington, A. | 555-1234 | Jazzercise | |
| 5  | Muncie, D. | 555-2345 | Walkercize | |
| 6  | Somerset, S. | 555-9876 | Slidercize | |
| 7  | Marion, C. | 555-8765 | Walkercize | |
| 8  | Wabash, P. | 555-6789 | Walkercize | |
| 9  | Van Buren, J. | 555-0101 | Slidercize | |
| 10 | LaFontaine, D. | 555-3131 | Bikercize | |
| 11 | Banquo, G. | 555-0908 | Slidercize | |
| 12 | | | | |

# ACTIVITY 84

# Creating and Using Macros

## OBJECTIVE

**Estimated Time: 30 minutes**

• Automate work with macros

For the last day of school, McMillan Middle School has a field day. You are dividing the entire eighth grade class into teams of 10. You create a roster of all the teams on a spreadsheet. To save time, you write a macro that creates a numeric list 1 through 10 and centers the numbers. You write another macro that puts the titles Last Name and First Name in the next two columns.

## INSTRUCTIONS

1. Create a new spreadsheet.

2. The results of both macros are shown below. Refer to this sample as you complete steps 3 through 6.

3. Create a macro that numbers 1 through 10 and centers the numbers. Name it **n**.

4. Create a macro that creates and centers the column headings **Last Name** and **First Name**. Name it **h**.

5. Save the spreadsheet as ACT084.

6. Use the macros to create numbers and column headings for five teams.

7. Save the spreadsheet again.

8. Close the file.

| | A | B | C |
|---|---|---|---|
| 1 | | Last Name | First Name |
| 2 | 1 | | |
| 3 | 2 | | |
| 4 | 3 | | |
| 5 | 4 | | |
| 6 | 5 | | |
| 7 | 6 | | |
| 8 | 7 | | |
| 9 | 8 | | |
| 10 | 9 | | |
| 11 | 10 | | |

# ACTIVITY 85

# Creating and Using Macros

## OBJECTIVE

• Design a macro to print and close a file

At the end of each week, you update your spreadsheet for the number of customer service calls that you have handled. You must send this weekly report to your supervisor. Therefore, after you update the spreadsheet, you must print and save it. Since you repeat these tasks weekly, you decide to write a macro that will print the spreadsheet, save it, and then close it.

## INSTRUCTIONS

1. Create a new spreadsheet.
2. Key the data shown below.
3. Create a macro that will (1) print range A1 to B8, (2) save the worksheet as ACT085, then (3) close the file.
4. Run the macro.
5. Save the spreadsheet as ACT085, if necessary.
6. Close the spreadsheet.

|   | A | B | C | D | E |
|---|---|---|---|---|---|
| 1 | Customer Service Calls | | | | |
| 2 | | | | | |
| 3 | Day | Number | | | |
| 4 | Monday | 41 | | | |
| 5 | Tuesday | 32 | | | |
| 6 | Wednesday | 37 | | | |
| 7 | Thursday | 49 | | | |
| 8 | Friday | 54 | | | |
| 9 | | | | | |

# ACTIVITY 86     Using Multiple Sheets/Tabbed Worksheets

## OBJECTIVES

**Estimated Time:  40 minutes**

♦ Create and name tabbed sheets
♦ Copy information for one sheet to another

    You are a member of an astronomers club. You have decided to create a spreadsheet that has multiple sheets, one sheet for each planet. You will start keeping information on each planet.

## INSTRUCTIONS

1. Create a new spreadsheet.

2. Create nine sheets within the spreadsheet. Name each sheet a name of a planet. (Hint: See below for a list of the planets.)

3. Enter the headings shown below for rows 1 and 2. Make sure each sheet has a set of headings. (Hint: Don't forget the copy and paste features.)

4. For each appropriate tab enter the data shown below on row 4. (For example, on the Earth's sheet, enter the information for Earth on row 4.) When you are done, you should have 9 sheets with the information for one planet on row 4 of each sheet.

5. Use the time format showing hours and minutes for the length of day data. Enter the range of temperature information as right aligned text.

6. Save the spreadsheet as ACT086.

7. Close the file.

| | A | B | C | D | E | F | G |
|---|---|---|---|---|---|---|---|
| 1 | Planet | Distance from Sun | Diameter | Length of Year | Length of Day | Range of Temperatures | # of Moons |
| 2 | | (Millions of Miles) | (Miles) | (Earth Days) | (Earth Hours) | (Degrees F) | |
| 3 | | | | | | | |
| 4 | Mercury | 36 | 3,031 | 88 | 1416:00 | -279/+801 | 0 |
| 4 | Venus | 67 | 7,521 | 225 | 5832:00 | +864 | 0 |
| 4 | Earth | 93 | 7,926 | 365 | 24:00 | -127/+136 | 1 |
| 4 | Mars | 141 | 4,223 | 687 | 24:37 | -225/+63 | 2 |
| 4 | Jupiter | 484 | 88,846 | 4,333 | 09:55 | -234 | 16 |
| 4 | Saturn | 888 | 74,898 | 10,759 | 10:39 | -288 | 18 |
| 4 | Uranus | 1,786 | 31,763 | 30,685 | 17:08 | -357 | 15 |
| 4 | Neptune | 2,799 | 30,800 | 60,190 | 16:07 | -353 | 8 |
| 4 | Pluto | 3,666 | 1,430 | 90,800 | 144:00 | -387/-369 | 1 |

# ACTIVITY 87     Linking Multiple Sheets/Tabbed Worksheets

## OBJECTIVE

**Estimated Time:  30 minutes**

• Link data between worksheets

At the end of each year you close a worksheet which has the ending price of each of the stocks in your investment portfolio. Then, you start a new worksheet to track the stocks for the next year. The closing price of each stock from one year becomes the beginning price of the stock for the next year. You need to bring the closing price of each stock forward to the new worksheet.

## INSTRUCTIONS

1. Create two spreadsheets, name one of them LASTYEAR and the other THISYEAR.

2. Key the data shown below.

3. Write a formula in cell B4 of the THISYEAR worksheet which will link to cell B4 of the LASTYEAR worksheet.

4. Repeat the process for cells B5 through B7 in the THISYEAR worksheet, linking to cells B5 through B7 of the LASTYEAR worksheet.

5. Save the spreadsheets.

6. Close both spreadsheets.

|   | A | B |
|---|---|---|
| 1 | Stock Tracker - Last Year | |
| 2 | | |
| 3 | Stock | Ending Price |
| 4 | Alpha Co. | 24.25 |
| 5 | Beta Co. | 17.50 |
| 6 | Gamma Co. | 44.75 |
| 7 | Delta Co. | 33.13 |
| 8 | | |

|   | A | B |
|---|---|---|
| 1 | Stock Tracker - Current Year | |
| 2 | | |
| 3 | Stock | Last Year's Close |
| 4 | Alpha Co. | |
| 5 | Beta Co. | |
| 6 | Gamma Co. | |
| 7 | Delta Co. | |
| 8 | | |

# ACTIVITY 88                    Changing Data in Linked Sheets

## OBJECTIVE                                      Estimated Time:  10 minutes

• Change text format in linked sheets

You are ready to print out your spreadsheet for the astronomers club. You want to quickly change the column titles to bold face. You do this by linking the sheets.

## INSTRUCTIONS

1. Open ACT086. (You must complete Activity 86 before continuing with this activity.)

2. Link all the sheets.

3. Select the cells that contain the column headings and change them to bold.

4. Adjust column widths as necessary.

5. Move to another sheet to verify that the link worked correctly.

6. Save the spreadsheet as ACT088.

7. Print the sheets for Mercury, Venus, Earth, and Mars.

8. Close the file.

# ACTIVITY 89

## Changing Data in Linked Sheets

### OBJECTIVE

**Estimated Time: 15 minutes**

* Update source data in linked sheets

You made a mistake when posting last year's closing prices of your stock portfolio. You need to update the values so that they are correct in this year's worksheet.

### INSTRUCTIONS

1. Open the spreadsheets you created in Activity 87 (LASTYEAR and THISYEAR). (You must complete Activity 87 before continuing with this activity.)

2. Change the value in cell B4 in the LASTYEAR worksheet from 24.25 to **20.20** and confirm that the value has been updated in cell B4 of the THISYEAR worksheet.

3. Change the value in cell B5 in the LASTYEAR worksheet from 17.50 to **25.25** and confirm that the value has been updated in cell B5 of the THISYEAR worksheet.

4. Change the value in cell B6 in the LASTYEAR worksheet from 44.75 to **50.50** and confirm that the value has been updated in cell B6 of the THISYEAR worksheet.

5. Change the value in cell B7 in the LASTYEAR worksheet from 33.13 to **30.30** and confirm that the value has been updated in cell B7 of the THISYEAR worksheet.

6. Print both revised spreadsheets.

7. Resave both spreadsheets.

8. Close both spreadsheets.

# ACTIVITY 90

# Using Backsolver/Goal Seek

## OBJECTIVE

**Estimated Time: 30 minutes**

• Use goal seeking to find a target value

Normally at the end of each year, you divide 10% of your company's profits among the employees. This year, however, has been an exceptionally good year, and you and your partners decide to give the employees a larger percentage of the profits without exceeding a target dollar amount. You and your partners will meet to decide what the percentage will be. They have asked you to prepare several scenarios for their consideration.

## INSTRUCTIONS

1. Create a new spreadsheet.
2. Key the data shown on the next page.
3. In cell B5 enter the following formula: **+B3*B4**.
4. Format cell B4 for percent with two decimal places.
5. Print the spreadsheet.
6. Use Goal Seek to determine the *Bonus Percentage* that would make the *Total to be Shared* equal to $30,000.
7. Print the spreadsheet.
8. Use Goal Seek again to determine the *Bonus Percentage* that would make the *Total to be Shared* equal to $40,000.
9. Print the spreadsheet.
10. Save the spreadsheet as ACT090.
11. Close the spreadsheet.

| | A | B | D | E |
|---|---|---|---|---|
| 1 | Bonus Calculator | | | |
| 2 | | | | |
| 3 | Profit | $225,750 | | |
| 4 | Bonus % | 10.00% | | |
| 5 | Total to be Shared | | | |
| 6 | | | | |
| 7 | | | | |

# ACTIVITY 91                                                    Using Backsolver/Goal Seek

## OBJECTIVE                                          **Estimated Time:  30 minutes**

* Use goal seeking to find a target value

   You are going into business providing scuba diving lessons off the coast of Baja. You must purchase a boat, but your payments absolutely cannot exceed a specific dollar amount each month. You have negotiated the best interest rate and payment terms that you can with the local bank. Now you need to determine the maximum amount you can pay for the boat.

## INSTRUCTIONS

1. Create a new spreadsheet.

2. Key the data shown below.

3. In cell B5 enter the proper formula to calculate the monthly payment for the boat. (The result should equal $243.55.) Format cell B5 for currency with two decimal places.

4. You cannot afford more than $225.00 per month.

5. Use Goal Seek to make the Monthly Payment (cell B6) equal to $225.00 by changing the Boat Cost (cell B3).

6. Save the spreadsheet as ACT091.

7. Print the spreadsheet.

8. Close the spreadsheet.

|   | A | B | D | E |
|---|---|---|---|---|
| 1 | Boat Purchase Worksheet | | | |
| 2 | | | | |
| 3 | Boat Cost | $17,500 | | |
| 4 | Interest Rate (%) | 11.25% | | |
| 5 | Term | 10 | years | |
| 6 | Monthly Payment | | | |

# ACTIVITY 92

# Using Spell Checking

## OBJECTIVE

**Estimated Time: 10 minutes**

• Use the spell check feature

You want to change careers. You research the growth of the major industries. You find information that gives the estimated growth percentages from 1990 to 2005.

## INSTRUCTIONS

1. Create a new spreadsheet.

2. Key the data shown below as displayed. (Key the misspellings.)

3. Spell check your work.

4. Save the spreadsheet as ACT092.

5. Print the spreadsheet.

6. Close the file.

|    | A | B |
|----|---|---|
| 1  | Industry | % of Growth |
| 2  |  |  |
| 3  | Argiculture | 14% |
| 4  | Constructin | 26% |
| 5  | Finance, incurance, and real istate | 21% |
| 6  | Government | 10% |
| 7  | Holesale | 19% |
| 8  | Manufracturing | -3% |
| 9  | Mineing | -11% |
| 10 | Retale | 23% |
| 11 | Services | 40% |
| 12 | Transprotation and Utilities | 14% |

# ACTIVITY 93

# Adding Cell Notes (Excel Only)

**OBJECTIVE**                                          **Estimated Time: 10 minutes**

* Add a note to a cell

You and a friend in your chemistry class are working together to develop a spreadsheet of the boiling and melting points of various elements. Since he will be adding the next group of elements, you decide to add a note reminding him to use Fahrenheit.

## INSTRUCTIONS

1. Open spreadsheet ACT080 or key the data shown below.

2. In cells B1 and C1, add the note, **Use Fahrenheit.**

3. Save the spreadsheet as ACT093.

4. Close the file.

|    | A        | B             | C             |
|----|----------|---------------|---------------|
| 1  | **Element**  | **Melting Point** | **Boiling Point** |
| 2  | Aluminum | 1220          | 4473          |
| 3  | Calcium  | 1542          | 2703          |
| 4  | Copper   | 1981          | 4653          |
| 5  | Gold     | 1947          | 5086          |
| 6  | Hydrogen | -434          | -423          |
| 7  | Iron     | 2795          | 4982          |
| 8  | Mercury  | -38           | 675           |
| 9  | Nickel   | 2647          | 4950          |
| 10 | Nitrogen | -346          | -321          |
| 11 | Oxygen   | -360          | -297          |
| 12 | Silver   | 1764          | 4014          |
| 13 | Tin      | 450           | 4118          |
| 14 | Uranium  | 2070          | 6904          |

# ACTIVITY 94

# Using AutoFill

## OBJECTIVE

• Fill a range of cells with incremental values automatically

You need to set up a worksheet to use for the upcoming year to track your quarterly sales of each of your products.

## INSTRUCTIONS

1. Create a new spreadsheet.

2. In cell B2 key **Qtr 1**.

3. In cell A3 key **Item # 101**.

4. Use AutoFill to fill cells C2 to E2 with the labels Qtr 2 through Qtr 4.

5. Use AutoFill to fill cells A4 to A12 with the labels Item #102 through Item #110.

6. Save the spreadsheet as ACT094.

7. Print the spreadsheet.

8. Close the spreadsheet.

|    | A         | B     | C | D | E |
|----|-----------|-------|---|---|---|
| 1  |           |       |   |   |   |
| 2  |           | Qtr 1 |   |   |   |
| 3  | Item #101 |       |   |   |   |
| 4  |           |       |   |   |   |
| 5  |           |       |   |   |   |
| 6  |           |       |   |   |   |
| 7  |           |       |   |   |   |
| 8  |           |       |   |   |   |
| 9  |           |       |   |   |   |
| 10 |           |       |   |   |   |
| 11 |           |       |   |   |   |
| 12 |           |       |   |   |   |

# ACTIVITY 95                Using AutoFill

## OBJECTIVE                    **Estimated Time: 30 minutes**

* Fill a range of cells with incremental values automatically

    You own Hank's Hot Dog stand and business is booming. You often need to compute the total price for products when they are bought in quantities greater than one. Therefore you are going to set up a spreadsheet that has pricing columns that you can print to make it easier to quickly calculate prices.

## INSTRUCTIONS

1. Create a new spreadsheet.

2. Key the data shown below.

3. In cell B2 key **1**.

4. In cell C2 key **2**.

5. Use AutoFill to fill cells B2 through F2 with values from 1 to 5.

6. Calculate the pricing for each of the items in quantities 2 through 5. Format the pricing cells for two decimal places.

7. Save the spreadsheet as ACT095.

8. Print the spreadsheet.

9. Close the spreadsheet.

|   | A | B | C | D | E | F | G |
|---|---|---|---|---|---|---|---|
| 1 | Pricing Table | | | | | | |
| 2 | | 1 | 2 | | | | |
| 3 | Hot Dogs | 1.19 | | | | | |
| 4 | Hamburgers | 1.59 | | | | | |
| 5 | French Fries | .79 | | | | | |
| 6 | Cola | 1.09 | | | | | |
| 7 | Coffee | .89 | | | | | |
| 8 | Chips | .49 | | | | | |
| 9 | | | | | | | |

# ACTIVITY 96

# Transposing Columns and Rows

**OBJECTIVE**

**Estimated Time: 10 minutes**

* Transpose columns and rows

Your boss wants to see a summary of the sales results of each department for the first half of the year.

**INSTRUCTIONS**

1. Create a new spreadsheet.

2. Key the data shown below.

3. Transpose the columns and rows so that Departments are in rows and months are column heads.

4. Determine the total sales for each department in column H. Add an appropriate column heading.

5. Save the spreadsheet as ACT096.

6. Print the spreadsheet.

7. Close the spreadsheet.

|   | A | B | C | D | E |
|---|---|---|---|---|---|
| 1 | Departmental Sales Results | | | | |
| 2 | | | | | |
| 3 | | Dept. 1 | Dept. 2 | Dept. 3 | Dept. 4 |
| 4 | Jan | 27894 | 31561 | 30056 | 29751 |
| 5 | Feb | 28942 | 30876 | 29156 | 28976 |
| 6 | Mar | 29114 | 30557 | 29617 | 29510 |
| 7 | Apr | 27937 | 31247 | 29337 | 30167 |
| 8 | May | 30004 | 31089 | 30173 | 29119 |
| 9 | Jun | 29994 | 29883 | 30654 | 29268 |

# ACTIVITY 97        Transposing Columns and Rows

## OBJECTIVE

**Estimated Time: 10 minutes**

◆ Transpose columns and rows

You have set up a spreadsheet in a vertical fashion and you think it would look better if it were horizontally arranged.

## INSTRUCTIONS

1. Create a new spreadsheet.
2. Key the data as shown below.
3. Transpose the range A2 through A4 into a horizontal arrangement starting in cell B1.
4. Save the spreadsheet as ACT097.
5. Close the worksheet.

| | A | B | C | D | E |
|---|---|---|---|---|---|
| 1 | | | | | |
| 2 | Jan | | | | |
| 3 | Feb | | | | |
| 4 | Mar | | | | |
| 5 | | | | | |

# ACTIVITY 98

# Using Zoom

## OBJECTIVE

**Estimated Time: 10 minutes**

• Use the zoom feature

You notice that the family budget that you set up in Activity 50 does not fit on the screen. If you could reduce the viewing size, you could read most of the spreadsheet without scrolling. You use the zoom feature to see more of the spreadsheet.

## INSTRUCTIONS

1. Open spreadsheet ACT050. (You must complete Activity 50 before continuing with this activity.)

2. Zoom to 75 percent. Notice that most of the spreadsheet is visible, and you can still read the data.

3. Zoom back to 100 percent.

4. Close the file without saving it.

# ACTIVITY 99

Review

## OBJECTIVE

**Estimated Time: 30 minutes**

♦ Review topics presented in Activities 52-98

## INSTRUCTIONS

1.  Create a new spreadsheet.
2.  Key the data shown in rows 1 through 3 of the spreadsheet on the next page.
3.  Use AutoFill to complete the proper month sequencing cells C3 and D3.
4.  Write the appropriate formula in cell E4, then copy it to cells E5 through E8.
5.  Write a formula in cell F4 that will calculate the bonus due to each person by multiplying their individual totals in the "E" column by cell E1. (Note: Write the formula using absolute references so that the formula will copy properly.) Format cell F4 for currency with 2 decimal places.
6.  Copy the formula in cell F4 to cells F5 through F8.
7.  Write the appropriate formula in cell B10, then copy it to cells C10 through F10.
8.  Write the appropriate formula in cell B11, then copy it to cells C11 through F11.
9.  Use Goal Seek to change the Bonus % (cell E1) to the proper percentage to make the Grand Total (cell F10) of all bonuses equal to $10,000.
10. Change formatting of titles and column headings as desired.
11. Create a bar chart to display the monthly totals for each person.
12. Save the spreadsheet as ACT099.
13. Print the spreadsheet.
14. Close the worksheet.

|    | A                    | B       | C    | D       | E        | F     |
|----|----------------------|---------|------|---------|----------|-------|
| 1  | Performance Analysis |         |      | Bonus % | 12.5%    |       |
| 2  |                      |         |      |         |          |       |
| 3  |                      | January |      |         | Q1 Total | Bonus |
| 4  | Davis                | 4575    | 3250 | 4150    |          |       |
| 5  | Johnson              | 3700    | 3825 | 4250    |          |       |
| 6  | Collins              | 5550    | 7250 | 4875    |          |       |
| 7  | Biggio               | 6525    | 4550 | 10250   |          |       |
| 8  | Martin               | 4500    | 3950 | 4725    |          |       |
| 9  |                      |         |      |         |          |       |
| 10 | Total                |         |      |         |          |       |
| 11 | Average              |         |      |         |          |       |

# ACTIVITY 100

# Create Your Own

## OBJECTIVES

- Change column widths
- Change text appearance
- Change row height
- Use a function
- Create a chart
- Use database functions
- Use spell check
- Use multiple sheets (optional)

You have a large cassette tape/compact disc library. You design a database to store information on your tape/CD library.

## INSTRUCTIONS

1. Create a new spreadsheet.

2. Enter the headings shown in the example on the next page. Make the headings bold face and centered both vertically and horizontally. Adjust the height of row 1.

3. Adjust column widths so that the data will fit.

4. Fill in the data from your personal library.

5. Use your own categories in the Style column. You can be as general or as precise as you want.

6. Format the Price column for currency with two decimal places.

7. Sort your database according to artist.

8. Now sort your database according to style.

9. Create query results on each category of the style. Perform a count on each query result. The formulas should be placed at the bottom of the database.

10. Create a pie chart that reflects the percentages of each count of the above styles.

11. (Optional) You are satisfied with the results of this inventory. Create another sheet behind this one and start an inventory for your VCR collection. Create your own headings that are useful to you.

12. Save the spreadsheet and chart as ACT100.

13. Print the spreadsheet and chart.

14. Close the chart and spreadsheet.

|   | A | B | C | D |
|---|---|---|---|---|
| 1 | **Tape/CD Name** | **Artist(s)** | **Style** | **Price** |
| 2 | | | | |
| 3 | | | | |

# NOTES

# NOTES

**NOTES**

# NOTES

# NOTES

# NOTES